SWEET & SIMPLE
GLUTEN-FREE BAKING

Irresistible Classics in 10 Ingredients or Less!

Sweet & Simple Gluten-Free Baking

Irresistible classics in 10 ingredients or less!

CHRYSTAL CARVER

PHOTOGRAPHY BY MARY BERNSEN

*Scan this QR Code
to learn more about
this title.*

Sweet & Simple Gluten-Free Baking
Irresistible Classics in 10 Ingredients or Less!

Copyright © 2014 by Chrystal Carver
Photographs by Mary Bernsen

Additional images through BigStockPhoto.com: Decorative swirls © Anja Kaiser.
Square memos © Francesco Ridolfi. Rectangle Memo © Salexander2.

Publisher: Inkwater Press | www.inkwaterpress.com

Paperback
ISBN-13 978-1-62901-130-1 | ISBN-10 1-62901-130-4

Printed in the U.S.A.
All paper is acid free and meets all ANSI standards for archival quality paper.

1 3 5 7 9 10 8 6 4 2

Dedication

For my two wonderful, beautiful, sweet, inquisitive girls, Allison and Molly, thank you for test-tasting every recipe and being my true source of motivation. For my mother-in-law, Cindy, for encouraging me to never give up, and for my husband, Tim, for all your support, love and honest feedback.

Acknowledgments

A lot of time and love is put into a cookbook. It takes teamwork and dedication to pull all the elements together and deliver a finished product.

Thank you to all of my family and friends for encouraging me to take my recipes to the next level. Thank you to all of you who tested recipes, test-tasted treats and provided honest feedback.

Many thanks to my talented and beautiful photographer Mary Bernsen for taking the most amazing photos and to Tim Bernsen for all of your assistance with the photo shoot.

Thank you to my husband for helping me with our girls while I tested and baked and for allowing me to turn our kitchen into a crazy bakery on the evenings and weekends. Special thanks to my girls who told me every day that I was "the best baker."

TABLE OF CONTENTS

Indicates the recipe is either dairy-free or has a dairy-free option.

Brownies and Bars

Frostings

Indicates the recipe is either dairy-free or has a dairy-free option.

INTRODUCTION

*H*ow much time and money have you spent at the grocery store or the bakery searching for and purchasing something gluten-free? We are all busy in our own ways, working, taking care of or spending time with family, etc. It's frustrating sometimes when our bank accounts or our palates are penalized because we are gluten-free.

In 2008, my two children contracted a stomach flu that lasted for 27 days. After a full recovery, both had stomach pain and were very irritable. After several tests, including a food sensitivity test, it was determined they were both extremely intolerant to gluten.

We spent hundreds of dollars the first few months trying to find foods they would eat, only to throw most of it away. Hey, they were small children under the age of five and fell into the category of "picky eaters." I heavily relied on gluten-free products such as packaged cookies, mixes and pastas. We have come a long way with the gluten-free community in the last few years, but we are still paying a lot at the checkout stand.

When my children started school, they began attending birthday and classroom parties. I found myself grabbing a couple of gluten-free cupcakes every week at the bakery, spending as much as $4 per cupcake. Both my children would eat the frosting off the top and throw away the cupcake because they didn't like the texture.

I sat down one night and broke my grocery bill out by food type to understand how much I was paying for gluten-free baked goods and mixes. Some people get into the normal hustle and bustle of life and don't realize just how much they are spending. More than half our bill was spent on packaged gluten-free cookies, muffin and pancake mixes—and my children were still limited to what they could eat.

I want my children to enjoy all the flavors of life, including classic treats like key lime pie and pineapple upside-down cake, for which you can't find a mix. Both my husband and I work full-time and with our children being in school and participating in sports, we needed to find a solution that would work for our busy lifestyles. Baking and cooking have been a norm in my family for centuries.

My sister was a chef, and I have been an avid baker for several years. In 2010, I decided to take all of my favorite classic treats and transfer them to easy gluten-free recipes for our girls.

I started with all of their favorite treats and worked through all of my favorites as well. At first I tried the "easy" gluten-free recipes I found. So many people claimed that their recipes were easy. What I found were recipes with elaborate ingredients in them or too many ingredients. Being that we were the busy family we were, I needed them to really be easy. To me, "easy" means that the recipe takes less than 30 minutes to prepare and less than an hour to bake. There should be no more than 10 ingredients and no complicated steps.

When I could not find what I wanted in gluten-free recipe books, I started experimenting with the recipes that I had been making for years, trying to convert them to gluten-free. After a few successful attempts I realized it was easier than it seemed. Some recipes were easy to convert—others took me a while to figure out. I had to learn about the different properties of the ingredients we use, why certain ingredients provide the textures they do, and why others help foods rise. Once I understood the science behind some of the ingredients I was using, I realized I could make anything gluten-free.

I started baking gluten-free for our children, several of my friends and co-workers who are gluten-free. After about a year my mother-in-law asked me if I was interested in writing a cookbook. I really was just doing it for my children, friends and family. I wanted them to enjoy the classic treats without having to give up on flavor or texture.

Then a thought occurred to me: Why not? Really, how many people struggle with what we did? Everyone should know how easy gluten-free baking can be and be able to enjoy all the classic treats without spending hours in the kitchen or extra money at the checkout stand.

I'm really excited to share these recipes with you.

Just like any cookbook, you will have your favorite recipes and you will have the ones you make for family and friends. This cookbook is written to help you understand why some foods work the way they do, provide you with easy recipes and help you enjoy classic treats, gluten-free.

GLUTEN-FREE BAKING IS EASIER THAN YOU THINK!

*T*he first thing I want you to know is gluten-free baking is easier than you think—it goes back to the same science we used years ago to create recipes with wheat.

Gluten-free baking is all about what ingredients we combine to get the flavors and textures that we prefer. Can you substitute wheat flour with a gluten-free flour blend and get the same results? Yes, in many recipes you can! It all depends on the texture and flavor you prefer and what other ingredients you have in your recipe that supports the combination you need to get what you want.

I know what some of you may be thinking—that you don't have time to learn the science of food. Don't worry, you don't have to understand the science of food to use the recipes in this book. I did all the legwork and rigorous testing for you. I provide some information on how flours and binding agents work. The information provided only includes a fraction of what is available and is provided for your information only—not expected to be the basis for your baking.

I simply want to help you understand why some ingredients work the way they do so you know why your recipes work or fail.

You'll notice there are hundreds of recipes out there today for the same type of food. Take chocolate chip cookies for example. How many recipes can you find for the "perfect chocolate chip cookie."

The perfect chocolate chip cookie depends on two main things. The first is what you prefer. Do you want a crunchy cookie or a chewy cookie? Do you like your cookies flat or thick? The second is on the combination of ingredients. If you mix the right ingredients together, you will make your perfect cookie. It's all in the science of the food and what ingredients work well with each other.

When you bake cookies, cakes, brownies and bars—depending on the texture you are trying to achieve—you can use almost any gluten-free flour mix in replacement of wheat flour. It all depends on the flour to rest of ingredient ratio and what type of gluten-free flour mix you use.

Take a look at the section I provide on the types of gluten-free flour.

CELIAC DISEASE VS. WHEAT ALLERGY VS. NON-CELIAC GLUTEN SENSITIVITY (NCGS)

Please note I have no formal training, education or certifications in any medical field. The information I'm sharing is what I've learned from doing research for my family.

With that said, Celiac Disease, Wheat Allergy and Non-Celiac Gluten Sensitivity (NCGS) are treated similarly but are three different medical conditions. People with these conditions must remove wheat from their diet. Each one may have a different symptom then the other.

Celiac disease is an inherited autoimmune condition, where the body's immune system starts attacking normal tissue, such as intestinal tissue, in response to eating gluten. NCGS is an immune reaction, but not an autoimmune reaction. Wheat allergy is an allergic reaction that occurs after eating wheat. You might see reactions in the skin, mouth, lungs and even the gastrointestinal (GI) tract. Like other allergic reactions, symptoms of wheat allergy can include rash, wheezing, lip swelling, abdominal pain and diarrhea. Symptoms may be any symptom in the body, not only gut symptoms: headaches, fatigue, depression/anxiety, rashes, joint pain, weight loss/gain, reflux, chronic cough, etc.

NCGS is not thought to be immune mediated. GI symptoms with wheat allergy or NCGS may include gassiness, abdominal pain, abdominal distension, and diarrhea. These symptoms are usually transient. People with NCGS may experience different symptoms and may tolerate different exposure levels to gluten. For example,

some celiacs have an immune reaction to oats, even if they are certified gluten-free. People with NCGS usually can tolerate oats, and should still ensure they are certified gluten-free before consuming them.

It's important to note that people with celiac disease, wheat allergies or NCGS need to ensure there are no traces of wheat in the foods they eat. All food, ingredients and preparation areas need to be 100% wheat and gluten-free. When following a recipe in a book, always make sure each ingredient is certified gluten- and wheat-free.

Flour

Flour plays a big role in the texture in baked goods and provides structure. If you have high-protein flour, it's going to absorb water quicker. Less protein-rich flours and gluten-free flours don't come together unless you add more flour or binding agents to aid with moisture absorption. Depending on your flour ratio to other ingredients in the dough, you can make your baked goods chewy, crispy or crumbly. Different types of baked goods depend on different amounts and types of flour. For example, if you want a crumbly cookie or cake, your flour to fat ratio will be higher. If you want a chewy cookie or a fluffier cake, you will use less flour and more eggs and fat.

Milk

I recommend using full-fat milk when possible. The fat in the milk helps keep your baked goods soft. Any type of milk will add moisture to your baked goods and help extend shelf life. The proteins in milk enhance the structure of your baked goods helping to bind with other ingredients when absorbed. Milk also encourages browning, which occurs when sugars and proteins in your dough or batter interact during the baking process.

Sugar

Sugar does many things in baked goods. It adds sweetness, helps the cookies caramelize and aids in developing the texture by absorbing moisture in the dough. Sugar also encourages your baked good to spread as it melts. The proportion of sugar in most cookie recipes is high because it allows about half of the sugar to dissolve during mixing. The remainder of the sugar will dissolve when your cookies begin to soften and spread. Sugar helps with flavor, texture and moisture absorption.

Fat

Adding sources of fat to baked goods helps with moisture, texture and flavor. Have you noticed how some recipes call for cold butter and others call for softened butter? When you add softened butters and oils to your dough or batter, it coats and protects the flour from the liquid. This prevents the flour from absorbing all of the liquid and helps baked goods yield tender and less chewy results. If you use cold butter in your dough, it takes longer for the butter to melt and coat the flours.

More moisture is absorbed during mixing, and as the butter melts it creates larger pockets of air.

The combination of reactions yields a more cake-like cookie or fluffier cake. Unless your recipe calls for cold butter, use butter at room temperature.

Eggs

Eggs provide the moisture and protein needed to aid ingredients with binding. They help with structure and texture, yielding fluffy and moist results. Make sure to use eggs at room temperature when baking. Your eggs will disperse more evenly into the batter, making for even cooking and lighter texture. To bring eggs to room temperature quickly, run them under hot water for 30–60 seconds or soak them in a bowl of warm water for 10–15 minutes.

Salt

Salt balances sweetness and flavors during baking. Without this flavor enhancer, the secondary flavors in your baked goods will be overpowered when the sweetness of your other ingredients takes over. Salt also strengthens the protein in dough, making cookies chewier. It controls the fermentation rate of yeast allowing for an even rise. If you use salted butter, adjust the amount of salt called for in your recipe.

SOME OF THE MANY GLUTEN-FREE FLOURS

$\mathcal{R}$emember how I mentioned the science behind the food? Here is a big part of that science. Grains used in traditional baking such as wheat, rye and barley are made up of two basic components: protein and starch.

Gluten is the protein in wheat that strengthens and binds the dough in recipes. The starch in wheat acts as a thickening agent. In order to replace wheat flour with gluten-free flour you need to combine gluten-free flour with a gluten-free starch, and sometimes add a binding agent. It is not a one-to-one ratio. The amount used will depend on the gluten-free flour and gluten-free starch you use.

Gluten protein is what traditional recipes rely on to thicken dough and batters, and to trap air bubbles that make your baked goods light and fluffy. Guar gum and xanthan gum are binding agents often used in gluten-free recipes to achieve similar results.

Below are some gluten-free flours you will find in grocery stores. This list is not comprehensive and does not contain all gluten-free flours.

Also listed are tips on how to store each type of flour. Please note that there are several different instructions out in the world on how and where to store flours. The list below includes the most common ways and time frames for storing flours.

Most types of flour keep well in a sealed container in a cool, dry, and dark location. The original packaging used for many types of flour is fine for long-term storage as long as the package has not been opened. Once opened, the shelf life decreases. Many types of flour are now marketed in resealable plastic bags that increase shelf life.

The refrigerator is a very good storage area for flour, but the use of a sealed container is even more important to prevent the flour from absorbing moisture as well as odors and flavors from other foods stored in the refrigerator.

The freezer compartment can be used for long-term storage, but when using a sealed container or a freezer bag, make sure it's full to eliminate as much air as possible.

Amaranth Flour

Amaranth flour is made from the seed of the amaranth plant, a leafy vegetable. Amaranth seeds are very high in protein, which makes it nutritious flour for baking.

Storage: You can store amaranth flour in a sealed container in the freezer for up to six months.

Brown Rice Flour

Brown rice flour is heavier than its relative, white rice flour. It's milled from unpolished brown rice, so has a higher nutritional value and higher fiber than white rice flour.

Rice flours tend to be grainy compared to other flours.

Storage: Buying brown rice flour in bulk is

not recommended, as it is better used when fresh. You can store brown rice flour in a sealed container in the refrigerator for four to five months and up to a year in the freezer.

Buckwheat Flour

Buckwheat flour is not, despite its name, a form of wheat. Buckwheat is actually related to rhubarb. The small seeds of the plant are ground to make flour.

Buckwheat has a strong nutty taste so is not generally used on its own in a recipe, as the taste of the finished product can be very overpowering, and a little bitter.

Storage: You can store buckwheat flour in a sealed container in the refrigerator for two to three months and up to six months in the freezer.

Chia Flour

Chia flour is made from ground chia seeds. Highly nutritious, chia seeds have been labeled a "superfood" containing Omega 3, fiber, calcium and protein, all packed into tiny seeds.

Tip: If chia flour isn't readily available, then put chia seeds in a processor and whizz some. If used in baking, liquid levels and baking time may need to be increased slightly.

Storage: You can store chia seeds or chia seed flour in a sealed container in a dark cool place for several months.

Chickpea Flour
(also known as gram or garbanzo flour)

Chickpea flour is ground from chickpeas and has a strong, slightly nutty taste—it is not generally used on its own. Chickpea flour is high in protein and is especially good for gluten-free baking. It can also be used to thicken soups, sauces or gravies.

Storage: You can store chickpea flour in a sealed container in the refrigerator for two to three months and up to six months in the freezer.

Corn Flour

Corn flour is milled from corn into a fine, white powder, and is used for thickening recipes and sauces. Corn flour has a bland taste, and therefore is used in conjunction with other ingredients that will impart flavor to the recipe.

Tips: Be careful in the grocery store. Some types of corn flour are milled from wheat but are labeled corn flour. Always look to make sure the flour was not processed in a facility that processes wheat.

Storage: You can store corn flour in a sealed container in a cool, dark place for up to one year and longer in the freezer.

Cornmeal

Cornmeal is ground from corn. It is heavier than corn flour, and not generally interchangeable in recipes.

Storage: You can store cornmeal in a sealed container in a cool, dark place for up to one year and longer in the freezer.

Hemp Flour

Made from ground hemp seeds, hemp flour has a mild, nutty flavor.

Storage: Hemp flour can go rancid easily. Hemp flour is best stored in a sealed container in the refrigerator or freezer.

Millet Flour

Millet flour comes from the grass family, and is used as a cereal in many African and Asian countries. Millet flour can be used to thicken soups and make flat breads and griddle cakes. Millet flour isn't suited to many types of baking, and is not used in the recipes in this cookbook.

Storage: Millet flour can become rancid quite rapidly if it is not properly stored. It is usually best to grind millet as needed to ensure the best flavor. You can store millet flour in a sealed container in the refrigerator for two months and in the freezer for up to six months.

Oat Flour

Ground from oats, oat flour works wonders in gluten-free baking because it contains starches that help your recipes bind together. You need to take special care to ensure it is sourced from a non–wheat contaminating process.

Tips: Oat flour absorbs liquids more than many flours, so you may need to increase the liquid content of any recipe to which it is added. Oat flour readily substitutes into many cake and cookie recipes.

Storage: Oat flour goes rancid very quickly— either buy small amounts and use quickly, or store it in a sealed container in the refrigerator or freezer.

Potato Flour

Potato flour should not be confused with potato starch flour. Potato flour has a strong potato flavor and is a heavy flour, so a little goes a long way. Bulk buying isn't recommended unless you are using it on a very regular basis for a variety of recipes, as it doesn't have a very long shelf life.

Potato Starch

Potato starch is made by washing, sometimes cooking, and then separating the starch present in potato cell walls so it can be made into powdered or liquid form. Potato starch is neutral in taste and works well for thickening sauces, gravies, stews and soups. Potato starch absorbs and retains moisture well and yields cakes and breads light in texture.

Quinoa Flour

(pronounced "keen wa")

Quinoa is related to the plant family of spinach and beets. Quinoa has been used for over 5,000 years as a cereal, and the Incas called it the "mother seed." Quinoa provides a good source of vegetable protein. The seeds of the quinoa plant are ground to make flour.

Storage: Quinoa flour can be stored in a sealed container for up to six months in the refrigerator or freezer.

Sorghum Flour

Sorghum flour is ground from sorghum grain, which is similar to millet. The flour is used to make porridge or flat unleavened breads, and is an important staple in Africa and India.

Storage: This flour stores well under normal temperatures. Store in a sealed container in a cool, dark place up to two months and up to four months in the freezer.

Tapioca Flour

Tapioca flour is made from the root of the cassava plant; once ground it takes the form of light, soft, fine white flour. Tapioca flour adds chewiness to baking and is a good thickener. Tapioca flour is an excellent addition to any gluten-free kitchen.

Storage: Tapioca flour is a fairly resilient flour, which you can store at room temperature in a sealed container.

Teff Flour

Teff comes from the grass family, and is a tiny cereal grain native to northern Africa. Teff is ground into flour and used to prepare injera, which is a spongy, slightly sour flat bread. Teff is now finding a niche in the health food market because it is very nutritious.

Tips: Adding too much teff flour to baked goods can make them gritty and dry. When baking gluten-free, use teff flour as part of a gluten-free baking mix.

Storage: Teff flour can be stored in a sealed container for up to four months in the refrigerator or freezer.

White Rice Flour

White rice flour is milled from polished white rice, so it is very bland in taste, and not particularly nutritious. White rice flour is ideal for recipes that require a light texture.

Tips: Do not replace wheat flour with white rice flour one to one.

Storage: Store in a sealed container in the refrigerator or freezer for up to two years.

BINDING AGENTS

$\mathcal{X}$anthan gum, psyllium husk powder and guar gum are frequently called for in gluten-free recipes, and serve the same general purpose as thickeners and binding agents. You can use just one or the other—or sometimes for the best results, you can use them in combination together.

In recipes containing wheat, rye or barley, the protein (gluten) in the flours serves the same purpose as guar gum, psyllium husk powder and xanthan gum in gluten-free baking. Gluten protein is what traditional recipes rely on to thicken dough and batters, and trap air bubbles to make your baked goods light and fluffy.

Xanthan gum tends to help starches combine to trap air, while guar gum helps keep large particles suspended in the mix. Psyllium husk powder is used to combine moisture and help keep breads from becoming too crumbly.

Guar gum is good for cold foods such as ice cream or pastry fillings, while xanthan gum is better for baked goods including yeast breads.

I've used psyllium husk powder for both purposes. Foods with a high acid content (such as lemon juice) can cause guar gum to lose its thickening abilities. For recipes involving citrus you'll want to use xanthan gum or increase the amount of guar gum used.

There are no set rules on which one you use. You'll have to experiment to see what works best in your recipes. Many people with celiac disease and non-celiac gluten sensitivity react negatively to xanthan gum. For that purpose, you can use guar gum or psyllium husk powder in replacement of xanthan gum. My family tolerates xanthan gum, so I use it in my baking. Most packages of xanthan gum, psyllium husk powder and guar gum have recommendations for how much to use with the different types of recipes.

XANTHAN GUM OR PSYLLIUM HUSK POWDER

Cookies	¼ teaspoon per cup of flour
Cakes and Pancakes	½ teaspoon per cup of flour
Muffins and Quick Breads	¾ teaspoon per cup of flour
Breads	1 to 1½ tsp. per cup of flour

GUAR GUM

Cookies	¼ to ½ tsp. per cup of flour
Cakes and Pancakes	¾ teaspoon per cup of flour
Muffins and Quick Breads	1 teaspoon per cup of flour
Breads	1½ to 2 tsp. per cup of flour

ALL-PURPOSE GLUTEN-FREE FLOUR BLENDS

$\mathscr{G}$luten-free baking doesn't need to involve a lot of flour mixes, xanthan gum or guar gum. Baking can get expensive and confusing quickly. When I work with gluten-free flours, I rely on basic flour substitutions that give me the same texture and flavor as gluten flours.

You can easily make your own flour blends or you can purchase ready-made flour blends. I mix all of my flours because I like to know what's in them, and I have more control over the final product. If you choose to purchase a gluten-free flour blend, make sure to carefully read the ingredients so you know what you're putting into your product. In addition to developing and testing the recipes with the gluten-free flour blends I developed below, I've also tested my recipes using Bob's Red Mill Gluten-free Flour Blend and Arrowhead Mill Gluten-free Flour Blend. If you're not interested in mixing your own blend, both blends yielded similar results and delivered delicious treats.

When I bake, I prefer to use bean flours, rice flours, potato starch and tapioca flour. Some people don't care for bean flours. I believe if you have the right ratios and the right ingredients, you will not be able to taste the bean in the end product. Just in case you're not a fan of bean flours, I have included a bean-free all purpose blend.

The two nutritious blends below work best with most baked goods and are the foundations for each of the recipes in this cookbook. The smell, flavor and texture are almost identical to wheat flour. You'll notice there's no xanthan gum or guar gum in the blends. Not all recipes require a binding agent. In a good portion of the recipes in this cookbook, the combination and ratio of ingredients are strong enough to hold the baked goods together. There are a few recipes that are fragile that still call for xanthan gum or psyllium husk powder. If you would like to learn more about xanthan gum, guar gum or psyllium husk powder, please see the previous chapter.

ALL-PURPOSE GLUTEN-FREE FLOUR BLEND #1
YIELDS 8 CUPS
Works with all recipes in this book.

3 cups garbanzo-fava bean flour
2 cups tapioca flour
1 cup sorghum flour
2 cups potato starch (or corn starch)

Note: If you cannot find garbanzo-fava bean flour, mix 1½ cups of garbanzo flour with 1½ cups of fava bean flour for the same results.

ALL-PURPOSE GLUTEN-FREE FLOUR BLEND #2
YIELDS 6 CUPS
Works best with cookies, brownies, bars, tarts and pie recipes.

4 cups white or brown rice flour
1 cups tapioca flour
1 cups potato starch (or corn starch)

Directions: Carefully measure the flours one at a time into a large mixing bowl. Start by spooning the flour into the measuring cup, then emptying the contents of the measuring cup into a large mixing bowl. Mix well. Store your gluten-free flour blend in an airtight container or freezer zip lock bag in the refrigerator or freezer for up to six months. Always shake container or mix the flour before using in case the heavier flours have settled.

GLUTEN-FREE BAKING TIPS AND TECHNIQUES

Gluten-free baking can be a trial-and-error process. Here are some tips and techniques that can help you achieve successful results.

- Check that all your ingredients are gluten-free before you begin.

- Thoroughly clean all surfaces and baking tools before you begin.

- Before you bring gluten-free foods into your home, you have to clean the kitchen to safely remove anything that may contain gluten. Even a tiny crumb or some flour dust can contaminate gluten-free products.

- I recommend reading recipe instructions before you begin. This will help you understand everything required and visualize the steps.

- Always measure gluten-free flours by spooning the flour or the mix lightly into a measuring cup and leveling off the top with the back of a knife.

- Always mix the binding agents, such as xanthan gum or guar gum, into the dry ingredients before you add the wet ingredients.

- It is not necessary, but a best practice, to stir or sift flours, starches, gums, salt and yeast or baking powder together so everything is evenly distributed.

- If a recipe calls for dough to be refrigerated, follow those instructions exactly. The time in the refrigerator will allow the dough to stiffen and absorb more of the liquid so the protein structure can develop.

- Egg sizes vary. This affects the liquid to dry ratio in a recipe. The recipes in this cookbook are based on large eggs. Eggs at room temperature work best.

- Be careful when mixing eggs into melted butter; be sure that the butter has cooled enough not to cook the eggs.

- Some baking powders might contain gluten (although most don't) because they are cut with wheat starch. Purchase gluten-free baking powder to be safe.

- Some oats contain gluten. When baking with oats always look for the gluten-free label.

- Unless the recipe calls for something different, place pans in the center of a preheated oven.

- Depending on if you are using a glass pan or metal pan, baking pans may require more or less baking time. If a recipe states that the bake time varies, I start with the lowest time and watch the oven.

- Oven temperatures vary slightly from oven to oven. I recommend getting an oven thermometer to see where your temperatures check in at. Adjust baking times and/or temperature settings accordingly.

- Some recipes suggest using a food processor to cut butter into doughs and crusts. If you don't have a food processor, simply cut butter in with a pastry blender.

- I suggest letting your oven temperature stabilize for at least 15 minutes after the preheat cycle is complete, before baking.

- Baking at high altitude can be challenging when using wheat flour recipes. Liquids evaporate faster and gases in cakes and breads expand more quickly, requiring adjustments to ensure a good final product. When wheat flour is replaced with gluten-free flour blends, the same challenges remain. You will need to experiment with recipes, first making any necessary adjustments for the altitude change and then altering the recipe further as needed to adjust for the properties of the gluten-free flours. High altitude gluten-free baking usually requires a little less liquid (start with two tablespoons less) and a higher oven temperature (increase oven temp by 25 degrees F) or a longer baking time.

Baking Powder vs. Baking Soda

Baking powder and baking soda are used to leaven baked goods that have a delicate structure. They both work quickly, relying on chemical reactions between acidic and alkaline compounds to produce the carbon dioxide necessary to inflate dough or batter. Some recipes call for baking soda, while others call for baking powder. Which ingredient is used depends on the other ingredients in the recipe. The ultimate goal is to produce a tasty product with a pleasing texture. Baking soda is basic and will yield a bitter taste unless countered by the acidity of another ingredient, such as buttermilk. You'll find baking soda in cookie recipes. Baking powder contains both an acid and a base and has an overall neutral effect in terms of taste. Recipes that call for baking powder often call for other neutral-tasting ingredients, such as milk. Baking powder is a common ingredient in cakes and biscuits.

Baking Soda
Baking soda is pure sodium bicarbonate. When baking soda is combined with moisture and an acidic ingredient (e.g., yogurt, chocolate, buttermilk, honey), the resulting chemical reaction produces bubbles of carbon dioxide that expand under oven temperatures, causing baked goods to rise. The reaction begins immediately upon mixing the ingredients, so you need to bake recipes which call for baking soda immediately, or else they will fall flat.

Baking Powder
Baking powder contains sodium bicarbonate, but it includes the acidifying agent already (cream of tartar), and also a drying agent (usually starch). Baking powder is available as single-acting baking powder and as double-acting baking powder. Single-acting powders are activated by moisture, so you must bake recipes which include this product immediately after mixing. Double-acting powders react in two phases and can stand for a while before baking. With double-acting powder, some gas is released at room temperature when the powder is added to dough, but the majority of the gas is released after the temperature of the dough increases in the oven.

Substituting Baking Powder
You can substitute baking powder in place of baking soda (you'll need more baking powder and it may affect the taste), but you can't use baking soda when a recipe calls for baking

powder. Baking soda by itself lacks the acidity to make a cake rise. However, you can make your own baking powder if you have baking soda and cream of tartar. Simply mix two parts cream of tartar with one part baking soda.

Substitution Solutions

Many of our favorite baked goods often have dairy products or eggs as a base or staple ingredient. These helpful substitutions will aid you in creating dairy-free and egg-free versions of classic recipes that often contain milk, yogurt, butter and eggs. Not all of the recipes in this cookbook have been tested with substitutions. The recipes that have been tested and work well with substitutions have been noted on the recipe page.

Milk
Replace one cup cow's milk with one of the following:
- 1 cup soy milk (plain)
- 1 cup rice milk
- 1 cup coconut milk
- 1 cup almond milk

Buttermilk
Replace one cup buttermilk with one of the following:
- 1 cup soy milk, rice milk or almond milk + 1 tablespoon lemon juice or 1 tablespoon white vinegar. Let stand until slightly thickened.
- 1 cup coconut milk, 7/8 cup rice milk, ½ cup of plain regular Greek yogurt, + ¼ cup of milk, soy milk, rice milk, or almond milk.

Yogurt
Replace one cup yogurt with one of the following:

- 1 cup soy yogurt or coconut yogurt
- 1 cup soy sour cream
- 1 cup unsweetened applesauce

Butter
Replace eight tablespoons (one stick) of butter with one of the following:
- Fleischmann's unsalted margarine 8 tablespoons (1 stick)
- Earth Balance Buttery Spread 8 tablespoons (½ cup)
- Spectrum Organic Shortening 8 tablespoons (½ cup)
- Vegetable or olive oil 8 tablespoons (½ cup)
- Coconut oil

Eggs
Replace one large egg with one of the following:
- 3 tablespoons unsweetened applesauce + 1 teaspoon baking powder
- 1 tablespoon flax meal or chia seed + 3 tablespoons hot water. Let stand, stirring occasionally for 10 minutes or until thick. Use without straining.
- Egg Replacer, according to package directions

Note: Replacing more than two eggs will change the integrity of a recipe. Because egg substitutions add moisture, you may have to increase baking times slightly.

GENERAL MEASUREMENT CONVERSIONS

Americans typically measure ingredients by volume, while just about everyone else measures them by weight. Here is a quick summary of some of the basic measurement conversions. This list is not exhaustive, but it should help you try to work with measurements while using the recipes in this cookbook.

US Dry Volume Measurements

Measure	Equivalent
1/16 teaspoon	dash
1/8 teaspoon	a pinch
3 teaspoons	1 tablespoon
1/8 cup	2 tablespoons (=1 standard coffee scoop)
1/4 cup	4 tablespoons
1/3 cup	5 tablespoons plus 1 teaspoon
1/2 cup	8 tablespoons
3/4 cup	12 tablespoons
1 cup	16 tablespoons
1 pound	16 ounces

US liquid volume measurements

16 tablespoons	1 cup
8 fluid oz.	1 cup
1 pint	2 cups (=16 fluid ounces)
1 quart	2 pints (=4 cups)
1 gallon	4 quarts (=16 cups)

US to Metric Conversions

1/5 teaspoon	1 ml
1 teaspoon	5 ml
1 tablespoon	15 ml
1 fluid oz.	30 ml
1/5 cup	50 ml
1 cup	240 ml
2 cups (1 pint)	470 ml
4 cups (1 quart)	.95 liter
4 quarts (1 gal.)	3.8 liters
1 oz.	28 grams
1 pound	454 grams

*ml stands for milliliter, one thousandth of a liter

STOCKING THE PANTRY

Refrigerator and Freezer

Almond Milk
Apples
Bananas
Blackberries
Blueberries
Butter
Buttermilk
Coconut Milk
Cream Cheese
Eggs
Fruit Jam (sugar-free blackberry and strawberry)
Lemon Curd
Lemon Juice
Lemons
Lime Juice
Milk
Oranges
Peaches
Sour Cream
Strawberries
Whipping Cream
White Vinegar

Spices and Seasonings

Ground Allspice
Ground Cinnamon
Ground Ginger
Ground Nutmeg
Ground Pumpkin Spice

Peppermint Extract
Salt
Vanilla Extract

Cupboard

Baking Powder
Baking Soda
Brown Sugar
Butter Flavored Shortening
Candied Cherries
Candied Pineapple
Chocolate Hazelnut Butter
Coconut Flour
Coconut Oil
Coffee
Powdered Sugar
Cornmeal
Cornstarch
Craisins or Dried Cranberries
Cream of Tartar
Dark Chocolate Squares
Evaporated Milk
Fava Bean Flour
Flaked Coconut
Garbanzo Flour
Garbanzo–Fava Bean Flour
Gluten-Free Butterscotch Chips
Gluten-Free Chocolate Chips
Gluten-Free Oats
Gluten-Free Quick Oats
Gluten-Free Rice Crispy Cereal
Gluten-Free Vanilla Chips
Ground Almonds

Ground Flaxseed
Honey
Jars of Baby Food Carrots
Macadamia Nuts
Molasses
Olive Oil
Peanut Butter
Pecans
Pineapple Chunks
Pineapple Rings
Potato Starch
Psyllium Husk Powder
Pumpkin Purée (not pie filling)
Red Food Coloring
Shortening
Sorghum Flour
Sugar
Sweetened Condensed Milk
Tapioca Flour
Unsweetened Cocoa Powder
Vegetable Oil
Walnuts
White Rice Flour
Xanthan Gum

17

Cakes, Cupcakes and Breads

Angel Food Cake

Banana Muffins

Blueberry Muffins

Buttermilk Coffee Cake

Carrot Cake

Cake Donuts

Chocolate Chip Muffins

Chocolate Cupcakes

Chocolate Vegan Cupcakes

Cornbread

Donut Muffins

Lemon Bread

Pancakes

Pineapple Upside-Down Cake

Pumpkin Cupcakes

Red Velvet Cake

Strawberry Short Cake

Vanilla Cupcakes

Waffles

Angel Food Cake

The light flavors and fluffy texture associated with this cake make it very versatile. You can serve it with fruit topping, chocolate sauce, whipped cream—or enjoy it plain. One of my favorite ways to serve this cake is to top it with whipped cream, sliced strawberries and kiwi. Beautiful, easy and palate-pleasing.

INGREDIENTS

1½ cups all-purpose gluten-free flour blend

½ teaspoon xanthan gum or psyllium husk powder

½ teaspoon salt

1½ cups granulated sugar, divided

12 large egg whites

¼ cup warm water

1 teaspoon gluten-free vanilla extract

1½ teaspoons cream of tartar

METHOD

Preheat oven to 350°F (180°C). Position the oven rack on the bottom of oven, in the lowest position.

In a medium mixing bowl, combine the flour, xanthan gum, salt and ¾ cup of the sugar; set aside.

In a large mixing bowl, beat egg whites, water, vanilla extract, and cream of tartar on low speed until the mixture starts to thicken. Increase the speed to medium and slowly add in the remaining ¾ cup of sugar. Beat until medium peaks form (a peak will hold, but not stiffly).

Slowly add flour mixture, a little at a time, over the top of the beaten whites and fold to combine. Continue until all the flour has been incorporated. Carefully pour the batter into an ungreased tube pan with removable bottom. Cut gently through batter with metal spatula to break up air pockets.

Bake for 45 minutes or until the cake springs back when touched. Allow the pan to cool upside down on a wire rack. Once the pan is completely cool, run the knife between the cake and the bottom of the pan to release it. Carefully invert over a cake plate.

Serve plain or with fresh fruit. Store covered at room temperature.

> **BAKER'S NOTE:**
> Be careful not to over beat the angel food cake batter: it will cause the egg whites to deflate. Beat just until they form soft peaks.

Banana Muffins

PREP TIME: 10 minutes   COOK TIME: 25 minutes   SERVINGS: 15   INGREDIENTS: 8

These banana muffins have been a breakfast favorite in my house for years. My family requests at least a batch a week. They are easy to make, quick to bake, and store up to a week in an airtight container in the fridge.

INGREDIENTS

1½ cups all-purpose gluten-free flour blend

1 teaspoon gluten-free baking powder

1 teaspoon baking soda

½ teaspoon salt (omit if using salted butter)

1 egg

¾ cup granulated sugar

⅓ cup butter, melted

3 large bananas, mashed
(preferably overripe)

OPTIONAL INGREDIENTS

½ cup chopped walnuts, pecans or gluten-free
   chocolate chips

SUBSTITUTION SOLUTIONS:

Substitute the butter with dairy-free butter, coconut oil or margarine to make these muffins dairy-free!

METHOD

Preheat oven to 350°F (180°C). Position the oven rack in center of oven. Grease a 12-serving cupcake pan or line a 12-serving cupcake pan with paper liners; set aside.

In a medium mixing bowl combine flour, baking powder, baking soda and salt.

In a separate large bowl beat egg, sugar, melted butter and mashed banana. Add the wet ingredients to the dry ingredients and stir just until mixed. Fold in the nuts or chocolate chips if desired.

Spoon the batter evenly into each cupcake pan, about ⅔ full. Bake for 20–22 minutes or until a wooden toothpick inserted near center comes out clean. Store in an airtight container at room temperature.

Blueberry Muffins

PREP TIME: 10 minutes   COOK TIME: 25 minutes   SERVINGS: 12   INGREDIENTS: 9

These tasty muffins are quite the satisfiers when you're craving a fruit-inclusive treat. They can be consumed at breakfast or inhaled as dessert. Top one off with some whipped cream or lemon curd and you might decide to finish the batch in one sitting.

INGREDIENTS

1¾ cups all-purpose gluten-free flour blend

⅔ cup granulated sugar

2 teaspoon gluten-free baking powder

¼ teaspoon salt

2 eggs

¾ cup milk

¼ cup vegetable oil

1 teaspoon fresh grated lemon zest

¾ cup fresh or frozen blueberries

SUBSTITUTION SOLUTIONS:

Substitute the milk with rice or almond milk to make these muffins dairy-free.

METHOD

Preheat oven to 350°F (180°C). Position the oven rack in center of oven. Grease a 12-serving cupcake pan or line a 12-serving cupcake pan with paper liners; set aside.

In a medium mixing bowl, combine flour, sugar, baking powder and salt.

In a separate medium bowl, beat eggs, milk, vegetable oil and lemon zest. Add the wet ingredients to the dry ingredients and stir just until mixed. Fold in the blueberries.

Spoon the batter evenly into each cupcake pan, about ⅔ full. Bake for 22–24 minutes or until a wooden toothpick inserted near center comes out clean. Store in an airtight container at room temperature.

Buttermilk Coffee Cake

PREP TIME: 10 minutes   COOK TIME: 35 minutes   SERVINGS: 8   INGREDIENTS: 10

This rich, moist and crumbly cake is enjoyable at all hours of the day. The buttermilk, nutmeg and cinnamon come together, making this recipe irresistible to most. If this cake was any more scrumptious I might have to put a warning label on the recipe.

INGREDIENTS

1¼ cups all-purpose gluten-free flour blend

¾ cups brown sugar, packed

¼ teaspoon salt

⅓ cup butter, room temperature

1 teaspoon gluten-free baking powder

¼ teaspoon baking soda

¼ teaspoon ground cinnamon

¼ teaspoon ground nutmeg

⅔ cup buttermilk

1 egg

OPTIONAL INGREDIENTS

½ cup chopped pecans or walnuts

> ### SUBSTITUTION SOLUTIONS:
> Substitute the buttermilk with 1 cup dairy-free vanilla yogurt, and the butter with a dairy-free butter, to make this coffee cake dairy-free!

METHOD

Preheat oven to 350°F (180°C). Position the oven rack in center of oven. Grease an 8x8x2" pan; set pan aside.

In a medium mixing bowl combine flour, brown sugar and salt. Cut in butter until crumbly. Set aside ¼ cup of the mixture to reserve for the topping. Add baking powder, baking soda, cinnamon, and nutmeg to the remaining mixture. Mix until combined. Add buttermilk and egg and mix well.

Spoon the cake batter evenly into the pan. If desired, add chopped nuts to the reserved crumbs. Sprinkle reserved crumbs on top of batter.

Bake for 30–35 minutes or until a wooden toothpick inserted near center comes out clean. Store at room temperature.

Carrot Cake

PREP TIME: 10 minutes   COOK TIME: 45 minutes   SERVINGS: 24   INGREDIENTS: 10

Carrot cake has always been one of my favorite desserts. I enjoy the sweet flavor of carrots, the spice from the cinnamon and the smooth texture that is consistent with each bite. This cake is fluffy and moist. Don't be surprised if friends and family mistake it for the gluten-inclusive version.

INGREDIENTS

2 cups granulated sugar

4 eggs

1 cup vegetable oil

2 teaspoons gluten-free vanilla extract

2 cups all-purpose gluten-free flour blend

1 teaspoon baking soda

1 teaspoon gluten-free baking powder

2 teaspoons cinnamon

2 teaspoons xanthan gum or psyllium husk powder

2 cups freshly grated carrots

OPTIONAL INGREDIENTS

½ cup chopped pecans or walnuts

METHOD

Preheat oven to 350°F (180°C). Position the oven rack in center of oven. Grease two 9" round cake pans, or line three 12-serving cupcake pans with paper liners; set aside.

In a large mixing bowl, cream sugar and eggs. Add oil and vanilla; beat just until smooth.

In a separate medium mixing bowl combine flour, baking soda, baking powder, cinnamon and xanthan gum. Add the dry ingredients to the wet ingredients and mix until combined. Stir in grated carrots.

Optional: Stir in chopped nuts.

Spoon batter evenly into two round 9" pans or cupcake paper liners filling about ⅔ full. Do not overfill.

Bake for 45–55 minutes or until a toothpick inserted into the middle of the cake comes out clean.

Cupcakes: Reduce baking time to 30–35 minutes or until a toothpick inserted into the middle of the cake comes out clean. Cool on a wire rack.

Remove from oven and let cool in the pan for 5–10 minutes, then remove from pan and let cool on a rack.

Frost each cake or cupcake with your favorite frosting.

> **BAKER'S NOTE:**
> Avoid picking up a spice "mix" for baking, and opt for real cinnamon that you can adjust to taste.

NUTRITION PER SERVING: 232 CALORIES; 13 G FAT, 2 G PROTEIN, 25 G CARBS; 1 G DIETARY FIBER

Cake Donuts

PREP TIME: 10 minutes   COOK TIME: 12 minutes   SERVINGS: 12   INGREDIENTS: 8

You didn't think I would write a cookbook full of sweet gluten-free treats and leave donuts out, did you? My children and I like to enjoy a donut every Friday. It's our special treat for getting through the week. These delicious donuts bring the flavors of a bakery right to your kitchen.

INGREDIENTS

2 cups all-purpose gluten-free flour blend

¾ cup granulated sugar

2 teaspoons gluten-free baking powder

¼ teaspoon ground nutmeg

1 teaspoon salt (omit if using salted butter)

¾ cup buttermilk

2 eggs

½ cup vegetable oil

OPTIONAL INGREDIENTS

powdered sugar, cinnamon sugar, chocolate glaze

> ### SUBSTITUTION SOLUTIONS:
> Substitute the buttermilk with 1 cup of vegan sour cream and the butter with a dairy-free butter to make these dairy-free!

METHOD

Preheat oven to 425°F (220°C). Position the oven rack in center of oven. Grease donut pan; set aside.

In a large mixing bowl, combine flour, sugar, baking powder, nutmeg and salt. Add buttermilk, eggs and vegetable oil. Beat until combined.

Fill each donut cup approximately ⅔ full. Bake for 8–10 minutes or until the top of the donuts springs back when touched. Let the donuts cool in the pan for 5 minutes.

If desired, coat with powdered sugar, cinnamon sugar or chocolate glaze. Serve fresh.

Store in an airtight container at room temperature.

NUTRITION PER SERVING: 160 CALORIES; 3 G FAT, 3 G PROTEIN, 30.5 G CARBS; 2 G DIETARY FIBER

Chocolate Chip Muffins

PREP TIME: 10 minutes   COOK TIME: 15 minutes   SERVINGS: 12   INGREDIENTS: 9

Imagine a chocolate chip cookie sandwiched between two vanilla cupcakes. The result would be a chocolate chip muffin. They are rich, dense and amazing straight out of the oven. Dress them up with some frosting or dress them down by making mini-muffins. Either way you're sure to please someone in the room.

INGREDIENTS

½ cup butter (1 stick), softened

½ cup granulated sugar

1 egg

½ teaspoon gluten-free vanilla extract

½ cup sour cream

¼ teaspoon salt

½ teaspoon baking soda

1 cup all-purpose gluten-free flour blend

½ cup gluten-free chocolate chips

SUBSTITUTION SOLUTIONS:

Substitute the sour cream with vegan sour cream, the butter with dairy-free butter and the chocolate chips with gluten-free, dairy-free chocolate chips to make these muffins dairy-free!

METHOD

Preheat oven to 350°F (180°C). Position the oven rack in center of oven. Grease a 12-serving cupcake pan or line a 12-serving cupcake pan with paper liners; set aside.

In a large bowl beat butter, sugar, egg, vanilla, sour cream, salt and baking soda until creamy. Add flour and mix until smooth. Fold in chocolate chips.

Spoon the batter evenly into cupcake pans, about ⅔ full. Bake for 22–24 minutes or until slightly golden and a wooden toothpick inserted near center comes out clean.

Store in an airtight container at room temperature.

Chocolate Cupcakes

This is one of three recipes in this cookbook that uses more than 10 ingredients. It actually calls for 11 ingredients, but it was so easy I didn't want to leave it out. These moist chocolate cupcakes are rich and delightful, and pair well with any frosting. You can enjoy these any time of the year.

INGREDIENTS

2 cups granulated sugar

2 cups all-purpose gluten-free flour blend

¾ cup unsweetened cocoa powder

1½ teaspoons gluten-free baking powder

1½ teaspoons baking soda

1 teaspoon salt

2 eggs

1 cup milk

½ cup vegetable oil

1½ teaspoons gluten-free vanilla extract

¾ cup boiling water

SUBSTITUTION SOLUTIONS:
Substitute the milk with almond or rice milk to make these dairy-free!

METHOD

Preheat oven to 350°F (180°C). Position the oven rack in center of oven. Line two 12-serving cupcake pans with paper liners; set aside.

In a large mixing bowl, stir together sugar, flour, cocoa, baking powder, baking soda and salt.

Add eggs, milk, oil and vanilla; beat with a mixer on medium speed for two minutes. Stir in boiling water.

Spoon the batter evenly into cupcake pans, filling them about ⅔ full. Bake for 20–22 minutes, until a wooden toothpick inserted near center comes out clean.

Remove from oven and let cool in the pan for 5 minutes, then remove from pan and let cool on a rack.

Frost each cupcake with your favorite frosting.

Cakes: For a two-layer 9" or two-layer 8" round cake, grease each pan and bake for 40 minutes for a 9" round or 35 minutes for an 8" round.

Remove from oven and let cool in the pan for 5 minutes, then remove from pan and let cool on a rack.

BAKER'S NOTE:
Most cakes continue to bake when they first come out of the oven. Make sure to test your cake for doneness often, near the end of the cooking cycle.

Chocolate Vegan Cupcakes

PREP TIME: 15 minutes   COOK TIME: 20 minutes   SERVINGS: 12   INGREDIENTS: 9

These sweet and spongy vegan chocolate cupcakes have been a big hit at parties and in the office. The coffee brings out the rich flavors of the cocoa while the vinegar and baking soda create tiny bubbles to help the cake rise. They are so easy to make and use basic ingredients usually found in most kitchens.

INGREDIENTS

1½ cups all-purpose gluten-free flour blend

¼ cup unsweetened cocoa powder

1 cup granulated sugar

1 teaspoon baking soda

½ teaspoon salt

1 cup brewed coffee

1 tablespoon white vinegar

2 teaspoons gluten-free vanilla extract

6 tablespoons (¼ cup plus 2 tablespoons) olive oil

METHOD

Preheat oven to 350°F (180°C). Position the oven rack in center of oven. Line a 12-serving cupcake pan with paper liners; set aside.

In a large mixing bowl, vigorously whisk together the flour, cocoa powder, sugar, baking soda, and salt until there are no visible clumps.

In a separate medium bowl, mix together the coffee, vinegar, vanilla extract, and olive oil. Pour the wet ingredients into the dry ingredients and stir only until they just come together. The mixture should be thin and lumpy.

Spoon the batter evenly into cupcake pans, filling them about ⅔ full. Bake for 18–20 minutes, until a wooden toothpick inserted near center comes out clean.

Remove from oven and let cool in the pan for 5 minutes, then remove from pan and let cool on a rack. Frost each cupcake with your favorite frosting.

Cakes: For a two-layer 9″ or two-layer 8″ round cake, grease each pan and bake for 40 minutes for a 9″ round or 35 minutes for an 8″ round.

Remove from oven and let cool in the pan for 5 minutes, then remove from pan and let cool on a rack.

Cornbread

PREP TIME: 10 minutes   COOK TIME: 25 minutes   SERVINGS: 12   INGREDIENTS: 8

This cornbread recipe is slightly sweet and pairs well with most soups. The key to making the perfect cornbread is to not over-mix the batter. Once you add your wet ingredients, you want to mix just until combined. I recommend serving it hot with butter or honey.

INGREDIENTS

1 cup all-purpose gluten-free flour blend

1 cup gluten-free corn meal

¼ cup granulated sugar

1 tablespoon gluten-free baking powder

½ teaspoon salt

2 eggs

1 cup milk

¼ cup vegetable oil

> **SUBSTITUTION SOLUTIONS:**
> Substitute the milk with almond or rice milk to make these dairy-free!

METHOD

Preheat oven to 425°F (220°C). Position the oven rack in center of oven. Grease a 12-serving cupcake pan or a square 9x9x2" baking pan; set aside.

In a medium mixing bowl combine flour, cornmeal, sugar, baking powder and salt.

In a separate medium bowl, beat together eggs, milk and oil. Add flour mixture to wet mixture and stir just until blended.

Spoon the batter evenly into the square pan or cupcake pans, filling about ⅔ full.

Bake for 25–30 minutes or until a wooden toothpick inserted near center comes out clean.

> **BAKER'S NOTE:**
> I would not recommend using paper baking cups for the cupcake pan version of this recipe. The contact with the pan allows the cornbread muffins to rise better and creates that golden brown outer layer.

Donut Muffins

PREP TIME: 15 minutes   COOK TIME: 20 minutes   SERVINGS: 12   INGREDIENTS: 10

If you don't have a donut pan, or you're looking for a quick donut fix, you can make these sweet and fluffy muffins in 35 minutes or less. You thought donuts were fast food? Try eating them disguised as a muffin!

INGREDIENTS

1½ cups all-purpose gluten-free flour blend

1½ teaspoons gluten-free baking powder

½ teaspoon salt

½ cup granulated sugar for cupcakes, plus ¼ cup for topping

½ cup butter, softened for cupcakes, plus ¼ cup butter, melted for topping

1 egg

½ teaspoon gluten-free vanilla extract

½ cup milk

½ teaspoon cinnamon

> SUBSTITUTION SOLUTIONS:
> Substitute milk with almond milk and the butter with a dairy-free butter to make these dairy-free!

METHOD

Preheat oven to 350°F (180°C). Position the oven rack in center of oven. Grease a 12-serving cupcake pan or line a 12-serving cupcake pan with paper liners; set aside.

In a small mixing bowl, combine flour, baking powder and salt.

In a large mixing bowl, beat ½ cup sugar, butter, egg and vanilla extract with an electric mixer on high for 1 minute or until combined. Add flour mixture and milk and mix until combined.

Spoon the batter evenly into the cupcake pans, filling about ⅔ full. Bake for 18–20 minutes or until a wooden toothpick inserted near center comes out clean.

Remove from oven and let cool in the pan for 5 minutes, then remove from pan and let cool on a rack.

In a small mixing bowl, combine the remaining ¼ cup of sugar and the cinnamon.

Brush the top of the muffins with melted butter and dip them into the cinnamon sugar mixture. Serve fresh.

Store in an airtight container at room temperature.

Lemon Bread

PREP TIME: 15 minutes   COOK TIME: 70 minutes   SERVINGS: 12   INGREDIENTS: 8

I call this lemon bread my "summer dessert." It's so light, moist and lemony! I like to top it with vanilla ice cream and fresh strawberries. If you're looking for a new fresh way to make strawberry shortcake, I highly recommend making this bread. You won't be disappointed.

INGREDIENTS

1½ cups all-purpose gluten-free flour blend

1 cup granulated sugar, plus ¼ cup sugar for the glaze

1 teaspoon gluten-free baking powder

½ teaspoon salt

2 eggs

½ cup milk

½ cup vegetable oil

zest from 1 large lemon

juice from 1 large lemon

> ### SUBSTITUTION SOLUTIONS:
> Substitute the milk with rice or almond milk to make this dairy-free!

METHOD

Preheat oven to 325°F (165°C). Position the oven rack in center of oven. Grease a 4½x8½" glass loaf baking pan; set aside.

In a medium mixing bowl, whisk together the flour, 1 cup sugar, baking powder and salt.

In a separate medium mixing bowl, mix eggs, milk, oil and lemon zest. Pour the dry ingredients into the wet ingredients and stir only until they just come together.

Pour batter into the greased loaf pan. Bake for 60–70 minutes, until a wooden toothpick inserted near center comes out clean. Remove from oven and let cool in the pan for 10 minutes, then remove from pan and let cool on a rack.

In a separate small bowl, mix the remaining ¼ cup of sugar and lemon juice. Microwave for 30 seconds, remove from the microwave. Stir until sugar is dissolved.

Evenly spoon the lemon sugar glaze over the top of the lemon bread. Cool completely before slicing.

Store in an airtight container.

Pancakes

PREP TIME: 10 minutes   COOK TIME: 15 minutes   SERVINGS: 10   INGREDIENTS: 9

These pancakes are fluffy, moist and delicious. My kids beg me to make them every weekend. My husband doesn't usually eat pancakes, but I often see him sneaking a couple of these onto his plate. Make a double batch and freeze half to enjoy at a later date!

INGREDIENTS

1¼ cups all-purpose gluten-free flour blend

1 tablespoon granulated sugar

1 teaspoon gluten-free baking powder

½ teaspoon baking soda

¼ teaspoon salt

¼ teaspoon cinnamon

1 egg

1 cup buttermilk

¼ cup vegetable oil

> **SUBSTITUTION SOLUTIONS:**
> Substitute the buttermilk with dairy-free yogurt to make these pancakes dairy-free!

METHOD

In a medium mixing bowl stir together flour, sugar, baking powder, baking soda, salt and cinnamon.

In a separate medium bowl, combine the egg, buttermilk, and oil. Add the flour mixture all at once to the wet mixture and stir just until combined but slightly lumpy.

Do not over-mix.

Turn your nonstick griddle or stove on low heat.

Pour ¼ cup of batter onto a hot, lightly greased nonstick griddle or nonstick skillet pan.

Cook until golden brown and turn when pancakes have a bubbly surface and the edges are cooked.

Serve with butter, syrup or your favorite toppings.

> **BAKER'S NOTE:**
> If your pancake edges brown before you see bubbles appear in the center, you may have your heat too high. Try lowering the heat to allow the pancake to cook evenly. This will help the center cook at the same rate as the outside edges.

Pineapple Upside-Down Cake

PREP TIME: 20 minutes	COOK TIME: 30 minutes	SERVINGS: 12	INGREDIENTS: 10

This cake is naturally moist, flavorful and fragrant. It can be served as a rich breakfast, a light dessert or a classic treat at tea time. This cake is enjoyed most when served warm.

INGREDIENTS

For the Cake:

1⅓ cups all-purpose gluten-free flour blend

⅔ cup granulated sugar

2 teaspoons gluten-free baking powder

⅔ cup milk

¼ cup butter (½ stick), softened

1 egg

1 teaspoon gluten-free vanilla extract

For the Topping:

¼ cup butter (½ stick)

⅓ cup packed brown sugar

2 tablespoons water

16-ounce can pineapple rings drained and halved (use pineapple tidbits if making mini cakes)

OPTIONAL INGREDIENTS

6 maraschino cherries, halved

METHOD

Preheat oven to 350°F (180°C). Position the oven rack in center of oven. Grease an 8x1½" round cake pan; set pan aside.

For the Cake: In a medium mixing bowl combine flour, sugar and baking powder. Add milk, butter, egg and vanilla. Beat with an electric mixer on low speed just until combined; set aside.

For the Topping: Melt the butter in a small mixing bowl in the microwave. Add brown sugar and 2 tablespoons of water. Spoon the sugar/butter mixture into the pan. Arrange pineapple and cherries (optional) in the pan.

Spoon the cake batter carefully into the pan, trying not to disturb the topping.

Bake for 30–35 minutes or until a wooden toothpick inserted near center comes out clean. Cool cake in pan on a wire rack about five minutes. Loosen sides; invert onto a plate. Serve warm.

Mini Cakes: use a 12-serving cupcake pan. Divide the brown sugar topping evenly between each cupcake pan. Use pineapple tidbits instead of pineapple rings. Divide the batter evenly between each cupcake pan. Bake 20–25 minutes or until a wooden toothpick inserted near the center comes out clean.

NUTRITION PER SERVING: 242 CALORIES; 8 G FAT, 3 G PROTEIN, 39 G CARBS; 2 G DIETARY FIBER

Pumpkin Cupcakes

PREP TIME: 10 minutes   COOK TIME: 25 minutes   SERVINGS: 12   INGREDIENTS: 11

I remember when I tested the results of this recipe in the office. One of my co-workers, who is very particular about his baked goods, was completely speechless when I told him these were gluten-free. They are moist, fluffy and have just the right amount of spice. You can eat them plain or with cream cheese frosting.

INGREDIENTS

1 cup all-purpose gluten-free flour blend

1 teaspoon gluten-free baking powder

½ teaspoon baking soda

½ teaspoon salt

1 teaspoon cinnamon

1 teaspoon allspice

2 eggs

1 cup canned pumpkin purée (8 oz.), not pie filling

½ cup granulated sugar

½ cup brown sugar, packed

½ cup vegetable oil

METHOD

Preheat oven to 350°F (180°C). Position the oven rack in center of oven. Line a 12-serving cupcake pan with paper liners; set aside.

In a medium mixing bowl, mix the flour, baking powder, baking soda, salt, cinnamon and allspice; set aside.

In a large mixing bowl, whisk together eggs, pumpkin purée, sugar, brown sugar and vegetable oil. Add the flour mixture to the wet ingredients and stir until combined.

Spoon the batter evenly into cupcake pan, about ⅔ full. Bake for 20–25 minutes, until a toothpick inserted in the center comes out clean. Remove from oven and let cool in the pan for 5–10 minutes, then remove from pan and let cool on a rack. Frost each cupcake with your favorite frosting.

Cakes: Double recipe for a two-layer 9" or two-layer 8" round cake. Grease each pan. Bake for 40 minutes for a 9" round or 35 minutes for an 8" round. Remove from oven and let cool in the pan for 5 minutes, then remove from pan and let cool on a rack.

Red Velvet Cake

PREP TIME: 20 minutes   COOK TIME: 30 minutes   SERVINGS: 24   INGREDIENTS: 13

Okay, I know I cheated. This recipe has more than ten ingredients. It's so easy and delicious—I couldn't leave it out! This soft, flavorful, colorful, divine cake is too tempting to ignore. The flavors of cocoa and buttermilk, topped with cream cheese frosting, create a whole new category of enjoyment. Please forgive me!

INGREDIENTS

2 cups all-purpose gluten-free flour blend

1 teaspoon baking soda

1 teaspoon gluten-free baking powder

2 tablespoons unsweetened cocoa powder

1 teaspoon salt

2 cups granulated sugar

1 cup vegetable oil

2 eggs

1 cup buttermilk

2 teaspoons gluten-free vanilla extract

1–2 oz. red food coloring

1 teaspoon white vinegar

½ cup prepared plain hot coffee

METHOD

Preheat oven to 350°F (180°C). Position the oven rack in center of oven. Generously grease and flour two 8" or 9" round cake pans; set aside.

In a medium mixing bowl, whisk together flour, baking soda, baking powder, cocoa powder and salt; set aside.

In a large mixing bowl, combine the sugar and vegetable oil. Mix in the eggs, buttermilk, vanilla and red food coloring until combined. Stir in the white vinegar and hot coffee. Combine the wet ingredients with the dry ingredients. Pour the batter evenly into each pan.

Bake for 30–40 minutes, or until a toothpick comes out clean. Do not over-bake. The cake will continue to cook as it cools.

Let cool on a cooling rack until the pans are warm to the touch. Remove the cakes from the pans and let them cool completely on a rack. Frost with cream cheese frosting. Store in an airtight container at room temperature.

Cupcakes: Line two 12-serving cupcake pans with paper liners. Fill each cupcake liner ⅔ of the way full. Do not overfill. Bake for 22–25 minutes or until a toothpick inserted into the center comes out clean. This recipe can be cut in half for one round cake or 12 cupcakes.

NUTRITION PER SERVING: 202 CALORIES; 10.5 G FAT, 2 G PROTEIN, 25.5 G CARBS; 2 G DIETARY FIBER

Strawberry Shortcake

PREP TIME: 20 minutes   COOK TIME: 14 minutes   SERVINGS: 12   INGREDIENTS: 8

I grew up eating strawberry shortcakes—a favorite in our household. These shortcakes are old-fashioned, dense and delicious. I recommend smothering them with fresh sliced strawberries and serving them straight up.

INGREDIENTS

For the Shortcakes:

1⅓ cups all-purpose gluten-free flour blend

⅔ cup granulated sugar

2 teaspoons gluten-free baking powder

⅔ cup buttermilk

¼ cup butter (½ stick), softened

1 egg

1 teaspoon gluten-free vanilla extract

For the Topping:

1 lb strawberries

2 tablespoons granulated sugar

OPTIONAL INGREDIENTS

whipped cream or vanilla ice cream

METHOD

Preheat oven to 350°F (180°C). Position the oven rack in center of oven. Grease a 12-serving cupcake pan or line a 12-serving cupcake pan with paper liners; set aside

For the Shortcakes: In a medium mixing bowl combine flour, sugar and baking powder. Add the buttermilk, butter, egg, and vanilla. Beat with an electric mixer on low speed just until combined.

Spoon the batter evenly into each cupcake pan, about ⅔ full. Bake for 14–16 minutes or until a wooden toothpick inserted near center comes out clean.

Remove from the oven and cool on a wire rack.

For the Topping: Remove the stems from the strawberries, wash and slice them into a bowl. Add sugar and blend with a fork. Cover and refrigerate until ready for use.

When ready to serve, cut each cake in half horizontally. Spoon strawberry topping on top; add whipped cream or vanilla ice cream if desired.

Store the cakes in an airtight container at room temperature.

Vanilla Cupcakes

PREP TIME: 10 minutes   COOK TIME: 25 minutes   SERVINGS: 12   INGREDIENTS: 8

The best vanilla cupcake is one you can frost with any flavor of frosting. These cupcakes are dense, moist and buttery. You can frost them with vanilla, chocolate, lemon or cream cheese frosting. Each frosting flavor delivers different results, but all are enjoyable.

INGREDIENTS

1 cup granulated sugar

2 eggs

1¼ cups all-purpose gluten-free flour blend

¼ teaspoon salt

1¾ teaspoons gluten-free baking powder

½ cup vegetable oil

½ cup milk

2 teaspoon gluten-free vanilla extract

METHOD

Preheat oven to 350°F (180°C). Position the oven rack in center of oven. Line a 12-serving cupcake pan with paper liners; set aside.

In a large mixing bowl, beat sugar and eggs with an electric mixer at medium speed for one minute. Add flour, salt, baking powder, oil, milk and vanilla; beat at medium speed for one minute.

Spoon the batter evenly into cupcake pan, about ⅔ full. Bake for 22–25 minutes or until the center springs back when touched and cupcakes are very lightly browned.

Let cupcakes cool in the pan on rack for five minutes. Remove cupcakes from pan onto rack and cool completely before frosting. Frost each cupcake with your favorite frosting.

Cakes: Double recipe for a two-layer 9″ or two-layer 8″ round cake. Bake for 40 minutes for a 9″ round or 35 minutes for an 8″ round.

Waffles

I love waffles! Waffles are an easy batter-based cake that you cook in a waffle iron pan. You can serve them for breakfast with your favorite toppings, use them to make breakfast sandwiches, or freeze them for future palate-pleasing activities.

INGREDIENTS

2 cups all-purpose gluten-free flour blend

1 tablespoon granulated sugar

4 teaspoons gluten-free baking powder

¼ teaspoon salt

½ teaspoon gluten-free vanilla extract

2 eggs

1¾ cup milk

½ cup vegetable oil

OPTIONAL INGREDIENTS

For cinnamon waffles, add ½ teaspoon ground cinnamon to the flour mixture.

SUBSTITUTION SOLUTIONS:

Substitute the milk with almond or rice milk to make these waffles dairy-free!

METHOD

Preheat waffle iron. In a large mixing bowl, combine flour, sugar, baking powder and salt until mixed. Add in the vanilla, eggs, milk and vegetable oil. Mix just until the batter is smooth.

If necessary, spray preheated waffle iron with non-stick cooking spray. Pour mix onto hot waffle iron, approximately ¼ cup. Cook until golden brown. Remove waffle from waffle iron.

Top with your favorite toppings. Serve hot.

BAKER'S NOTE:

Make sure your waffle iron is hot and either non-stick or well oiled. Serving a smaller crowd? Cut this recipe in half!

Cheesecakes, Pies and Tarts

Apple Crisp

Apple Wrap Pie

Blackberry Cream Cheese Pie

Cheesecake

Chocolate Shortbread Tarts

Key Lime Pie

Lemon Blackberry Tarts

Mini Pumpkin Cheesecakes

Peach Cobbler

Pecan Pie

Pumpkin Pie

Strawberry Cream Cheese Pie

Chocolate Pie Crust

Classic Pie Crust

Mock Graham Cracker Crust

Apple Crisp

PREP TIME: 20 minutes   COOK TIME: 30 minutes   SERVINGS: 8   INGREDIENTS: 7

This dessert has a perfect balance of spices baked into tart delicious apples. Serve it warm with whipped cream or ice cream, and you have yourself an award-winning, restaurant-style dish!

INGREDIENTS

4 medium Granny Smith apples, cored, peeled and sliced

¾ cup brown sugar, packed

½ cup all-purpose gluten-free flour blend

½ cup gluten-free quick oats

1 teaspoon ground cinnamon

1 teaspoon ground nutmeg

⅓ cup butter, softened

OPTIONAL INGREDIENTS

vanilla ice cream, whipped cream

> **SUBSTITUTION SOLUTIONS:**
> Substitute the butter with dairy-free butter to make this dairy-free!

METHOD

Preheat oven to 375°F (190°C). Position the oven rack in center of oven. Lightly spray or grease an 8x8x2" square pan.

Spread apple slices evenly on the bottom of the pan. In a medium mixing bowl, combine the brown sugar, flour, oats, cinnamon and nutmeg. With a pastry blender, cut the butter into the flour mixture until it resembles coarse crumbs. Evenly sprinkle the topping over the apples.

Bake for 30 minutes or until topping is golden brown and apples are tender when pierced with a fork. Serve warm with vanilla ice cream or whipped cream. Store at room temperature.

Apple Wrap Pie

PREP TIME: 40 minutes   COOK TIME: 35 minutes   SERVINGS: 8   INGREDIENTS: 8

This quick and easy apple wrap pie is just as tasty as its full two-pie-shell cousin, the apple pie. It can be sliced up for an easy finger food treat at a party, or served up in a dish disguised with ice cream.

INGREDIENTS

Pastry for Single-Crust Pie:

1½ cups all-purpose gluten-free flour blend

¼ teaspoon salt (omit if using salted butter)

½ cup butter (1 stick), cold

4–5 tablespoons of cold milk

For the Filling:

⅔ cup packed brown sugar

⅓ cup all-purpose gluten-free flour blend

¼ teaspoon ground cinnamon

¼ teaspoon ground nutmeg

4 medium tart apples, cored, peeled and thinly sliced

OPTIONAL INGREDIENTS

vanilla ice cream, whipped cream

> SUBSTITUTION SOLUTIONS:
> Substitute with dairy-free butter and rice or soy milk to make this pie crust dairy-free!

METHOD

Preheat oven to 425°F (220°C). Position the oven rack in center of oven.

For the Pie Crust: In a medium mixing bowl, combine flour and salt. With a pastry knife, cut butter into flour. Add milk and combine. Add additional milk if needed. Dough should be moist and easy to roll.

Roll dough out on a gluten-free floured surface with a rolling pin until approximately 13″ in diameter. Place on an ungreased cookie sheet.

For the Filling: In a large mixing bowl, combine brown sugar, remaining ⅓ cup flour, cinnamon and nutmeg. Stir in apple slices.

Pour apple filling into the middle of the pastry shell, leaving 3–4 inches from the edge. Fold edges of the pastry making pleats or folds so it lays flat on the apples.

Bake for 30–35 minutes, or the crust is golden brown. Remove from the oven and cool on the cookie sheet.

If desired, serve with vanilla ice cream or whipped cream.

Blackberry Cream Cheese Pie

PREP TIME: 10 minutes   COOK TIME: 30 minutes   SERVINGS: 12   INGREDIENTS: 10

You can make this pie fresh during the summer or use frozen berries for a fun wintry treat. This pie is a shortcut between a blackberry pie and a cheesecake. With only 10 ingredients and a few simple steps, you will have yourself a classic treat in no time.

INGREDIENTS

For the Crust:

½ cup all-purpose gluten-free flour blend

½ cup gluten-free quick cooking oats

⅓ cup brown sugar, packed

¼ cup butter (½ stick), cold, cut into 1-inch cubes

For the Topping:

5 cups blackberries

½ cup water

3 tablespoons cornstarch

⅔ cup granulated sugar

1 tablespoon lemon juice

For the Filling:

8 oz. cream cheese, softened

1 teaspoon lemon zest

OPTIONAL INGREDIENTS

whipped cream, fresh blackberries

METHOD

Preheat oven to 325°F (165°C). Position the oven rack in center of oven. Grease an 8" pie pan, set aside.

For the Crust: In a food processor, combine flour, quick oats, brown sugar and butter and process until finely chopped (approximately 30 seconds).

Press pie crust mixture into the bottom of an 8" glass pie pan. Bake for 25–28 minutes or until it starts to brown. Remove from the oven. Crust will appear raised. It should flatten on its own. If it doesn't, press the crust with a spoon until it is even and flat.

For the Topping: In a medium-size saucepan, combine 3 cups of the berries with the water. Bring to a boil. Let cool, then strain to remove the seeds. Return the syrup to the saucepan. Stir in the cornstarch, sugar and lemon juice. Bring to a boil, stirring, and boil for two minutes. Set aside and cool.

For the Filling: When the syrup is cool, in a medium mixing bowl, blend the cream cheese and lemon zest until smooth. Add ¼ cup of blackberry topping and blend just until combined. Spread evenly in the baked crust. Top with the remaining 2 cups uncooked berries.

Pour the rest of the cooled, thickened syrup evenly over the berries. Refrigerate for one hour or more.

NUTRITION PER SERVING: 266 CALORIES; 15.5 G FAT, 3.5 G PROTEIN, 28 G CARBS; 4.5 G DIETARY FIBER

Cheesecake

PREP TIME: 20 minutes   COOK TIME: 15 minutes   SERVINGS: 16   INGREDIENTS: 10

This classic cheesecake recipe converted to gluten-free is going to take the gluten-free community by storm. For so many years I wanted to enjoy a slice of cheesecake without the after-effects of the gluten. Top this wonderful creation with any of your favorite fruit toppings and enjoy!

INGREDIENTS

For the Crust:

1 cup all-purpose gluten-free flour blend

1 cup gluten-free quick cooking oats

⅔ cup brown sugar, packed

½ cup butter (1 stick), cold, cut into 1-inch cubes

For the Filling:

2 8-oz. packages cream cheese

¾ cup granulated sugar

¼ cup milk

2 eggs

½ cup sour cream

2 teaspoons gluten-free vanilla extract

2 tablespoons all-purpose gluten-free flour blend

METHOD

Preheat oven to 350°F (180°C). Position the oven rack in center of oven. Grease a 9" springform pan.

For the Crust: In a food processor, combine flour, quick oats, brown sugar and butter and process until finely chopped. Press into bottom of the springform pan.

For the Filling: In a large mixing bowl, beat cream cheese with sugar until smooth. Beat in milk, and then eggs one at a time, mixing just until combined. Beat in sour cream, vanilla and flour until smooth. Pour filling into prepared crust.

Bake for one hour or until the sides are set and the center is still slightly jiggly. Store in the refrigerator. Serve cold.

Chocolate Shortbread Tarts

These buttery shortbread tarts are divine. The whipped chocolate filling (combined with the crumbly crust) makes them irresistible. No need to thank me. They're one of my favorites, too!

INGREDIENTS

For the Crust:

2 cups all-purpose gluten-free flour blend

½ cup granulated sugar

½ cup unsweetened cocoa powder

1 teaspoon xanthan gum or psyllium husk powder

1 cup butter (2 sticks), softened

For the Chocolate Ganache:

1½ cups whipping cream

2¼ cups (1 12-oz. bag) gluten-free semi-sweet chocolate chips

METHOD

Preheat oven to 325°F (165°C). Position the oven rack in center of oven.

For the Crust: In a medium mixing bowl, combine flour, sugar, cocoa powder and xanthan gum. Using a pastry blender, cut in the butter until the mixture resembles fine crumbs. Form mixture into one big ball.

Knead until smooth. Separate dough into six even balls, press dough evenly into 5- or 6-inch tart pans. If you don't have a tart pan, see the baker's note.

Bake for 12–15 minutes, or until firm in the center. Remove from the oven and cool on a wire rack.

For Chocolate Ganache: In a medium saucepan, bring whipping cream to a boil over medium heat, stirring frequently. Remove from the heat and add chocolate chips. Let stand for five minutes, then stir still smooth. Cool for 15 minutes.

Fill each tart with chocolate ganache. Let cool completely before removing from the pan. Store in an airtight container in the refrigerator. Serve cold.

> **BAKER'S NOTE:**
> If you don't have a tart pan, you can make mini tarts using a muffin or cupcake pan. Separate the dough into 12 even balls. Press each ball into the bottom of the muffin or cupcake pans. Bake for 10–12 minutes.

NUTRITION PER SERVING: 760 CALORIES; 46.5 G FAT, 8 G PROTEIN, 77 G CARBS; 2 G DIETARY FIBER

Key Lime Pie

PREP TIME: 20 minutes   COOK TIME: 25 minutes   SERVINGS: 12   INGREDIENTS: 9

Let's be honest, you will probably never find a gluten-free mix for key lime pie, and if you do, it's not going be the same as the original. The key is in the crust. Pun intended! This tart and tangy pie held together by a cinnamon-rich mock graham cracker crust will leave you speechless.

INGREDIENTS

For the Crust:

½ cup all-purpose gluten-free flour blend

½ cup gluten-free quick cooking oats

⅓ cup brown sugar, packed

¼ teaspoon cinnamon

¼ teaspoon baking soda

¼ cup butter (½ stick), cold, cut into 1-inch cubes

For the Filling:

1 (14 oz.) can sweetened condensed milk

3 egg yolks

½ cup key lime juice

OPTIONAL INGREDIENTS

whipped cream, vanilla ice cream

METHOD

Preheat oven to 350°F (180°C). Position the oven rack in center of oven.

For the Crust: In a food processor, combine flour, quick oats, brown sugar, cinnamon, baking soda and butter and process until finely chopped (approximately 30 seconds). Press pie crust mixture into the bottom of an 8" glass pie pan. Bake for 10 minutes or until it starts to brown. Remove crust from the oven. Crust will appear raised. Press crust with a spoon until it is even and flat.

For the Filling: In a separate medium mixing bowl, combine sweetened condensed milk, egg yolks and lime juice and beat until completely mixed.

Pour filling into pie shell and bake for 15 minutes or until the center is set. Cool pan on wire rack for 10 minutes. Refrigerate two hours. If desired, top with vanilla ice cream or whipped cream. Store in the refrigerator.

> **BAKER'S NOTE:**
> The faster you use your eggs, the less time any potential bacteria will have to multiply. You can refrigerate egg whites, when properly handled, in a sealed container for up to 4 days, or in the freezer for up to 12 months. Save the egg whites from this recipe for a later date and you can use them to make coconut macaroons!

Lemon Blackberry Tarts

PREP TIME: 15 minutes   COOK TIME: 30 minutes   SERVINGS: 12   INGREDIENTS: 6

You will not believe how simple these are to make. When your friends and family come over, and they make comments on how long you must have spent making them, just nod and smile. These tarts are easy, tangy, sweet—and pleasing to most palates.

INGREDIENTS

For the Pastry Shell:

½ cup butter (1 stick), softened

4 oz. cream cheese, softened

1 cup all-purpose gluten-free flour blend

For the Filling:

8 oz. cream cheese, softened

½ cup lemon curd

For the Topping:

8 tablespoons seedless blackberry spreadable fruit

4 teaspoons lemon juice

OPTIONAL INGREDIENTS

sifted powdered sugar

METHOD

Preheat oven to 325°F (165°C). Position the oven rack in center of oven.

For the Pastry Shell: In a small mixing bowl, cream butter and 4 oz. cream cheese. Beat in flour. Shape dough into 12 balls. With floured fingers, press the balls into the bottom and up the sides of a greased mini tart pan or 12-serving cupcake pan.

Bake for 25–30 minutes or the edges are light brown. Cool completely on wire rack.

For the Filling: In a medium mixing bowl, beat 8 oz. cream cheese and lemon curd with an electric mixer on medium speed until smooth. Divide filling among pastry shells, spreading evenly. Cover; refrigerate two hours or until well chilled.

For the Topping: Combine spreadable fruit and lemon juice; spoon over tarts before serving.

Add sifted powdered sugar over tops if desired.

Mini Pumpkin Cheesecakes

PREP TIME: 20 minutes   COOK TIME: 15 minutes   SERVINGS: 12   INGREDIENTS: 10

Just imagine a perfect gingersnap crust, topped with spicy and smooth pumpkin cheese cake filling. Add a little whipped cream and enjoy all the flavors of fall wrapped into one scrumptious treat.

INGREDIENTS

For the Crust:

1 cup gluten-free gingersnap crumbs (or leftover gluten-free gingersnaps, crushed)

2 tablespoons granulated sugar

¼ cup (½ stick) of butter, melted

For the Filling:

1 cup pumpkin purée (not pie filling)

1 teaspoon cinnamon

¼ teaspoon nutmeg

⅛ teaspoon allspice

12 oz. cream cheese softened

½ cup granulated sugar

2 eggs

½ teaspoon gluten-free vanilla extract

OPTIONAL INGREDIENTS

vanilla ice cream, whipped cream

METHOD

Preheat oven to 325°F (165°C). Position the oven rack in center of oven. Lightly spray or grease 12 mini cheesecake pans.

For the Crust: In a small bowl, mix gingersnap crumbs, sugar and melted butter. Divide the mixture evenly into 12 mini cheesecake cups, about 1½ heaping teaspoons per cup. Press mixture into the bottom of each cup. Bake crust 8–10 minutes or until set. Remove from the oven and cool.

For the Filling: In a small bowl, combine pumpkin purée, cinnamon, nutmeg and allspice; set aside. In a separate medium mixing bowl, beat softened cream cheese and sugar on medium speed until smooth and no lumps remain. Add eggs one at a time, beating well after each egg.

Mix in the vanilla and pumpkin mixture and beat on low speed until smooth and creamy. Divide filling evenly among cups. Bake for 18–20 minutes or until set.

Remove from the oven and cool on wire rack. When pan is cool, refrigerate for 2–3 hours before unmolding.

If desired, top with vanilla ice cream or whipped cream before serving. Store in an airtight container in the refrigerator.

> **BAKER'S NOTE:**
> When your cheesecakes have cooled, the best way to unmold the cheesecake is to separate the crust from the disk carefully with a thin knife.

Peach Cobbler

PREP TIME: 20 minutes   COOK TIME: 35 minutes   SERVINGS: 8   INGREDIENTS: 10

If peach cobbler is not considered a classic, then what is? Peach cobbler recipes have been passed down in my family from generation to generation. It's a delightful dessert you can enjoy using fresh peaches during the summer or frozen peaches during the winter. Serve it hot to hit the spot!

INGREDIENTS

Pastry for Filling:

½ cup granulated sugar

1 tablespoon gluten-free corn starch

¼ cup water

4 cups fresh or frozen sliced peaches

For the Topping:

1 cup all-purpose gluten-free flour blend

¼ cup granulated sugar

1 teaspoon gluten-free baking powder

½ teaspoon ground cinnamon

3 tablespoons butter, softened

1 egg

3 tablespoons milk

OPTIONAL INGREDIENTS

vanilla ice cream, whipped cream

METHOD

Preheat oven to 400°F (200°C). Position the oven rack in center of oven. Grease an 8x8x2" pan; set aside.

For the Filling: In a medium saucepan, combine ½ cup sugar, cornstarch, water and peaches. Cook on low heat until thick and starts to boil. Remove from the heat; set aside.

For the Topping: In a medium mixing bowl, mix flour, ¼ cup sugar, baking powder and cinnamon. With a pastry cutter, cut butter in until the mixture resembles coarse crumbs.

In a separate small mixing bowl, combine eggs and milk and add to the flour mixture. Stir just until combined. Batter will be thick and lumpy.

Pour peach filling into the 8x8x2" pan.

Drop the topping into 6–8 mounds on top of the peach filling.

Bake for 20–25 minutes, or until a toothpick inserted into the topping comes out clean.

If desired, serve with vanilla ice cream or whipped cream. Store in the refrigerator or at room temperature.

Pecan Pie

PREP TIME: 20 minutes   COOK TIME: 50 minutes   SERVINGS: 12   INGREDIENTS: 9

Pecan pie is my father's number-one go-to dessert for everything, including a little comfort food. You don't have to be from the South to know how to make a good pie!

INGREDIENTS

Pastry for Single-Crust Pie:

1½ cups all-purpose gluten-free flour blend

¼ teaspoon salt (omit if using salted butter)

½ cup butter (1 stick), cold

4–5 tablespoons of cold milk

For the Filling:

2 eggs

½ cup butter (1 stick), melted

1 cup brown sugar, packed

¼ cup granulated sugar

1 tablespoon all-purpose gluten-free flour blend

1 tablespoon milk

1 teaspoon gluten-free vanilla extract

1 cup chopped pecans

OPTIONAL INGREDIENTS

vanilla ice cream, whipped cream

METHOD

Preheat oven to 400°F (200°C). Position the oven rack in center of oven.

For the Crust: In a medium mixing bowl, combine flour and salt. With a pastry knife, cut butter into flour. Add milk and combine. Add additional milk if needed. Dough should be moist and easy to roll.

Roll dough out on a gluten-free floured surface with a rolling pin until approximately 10″ in diameter. Place dough into 9″ pie pan and trim edges if necessary. Bake for 10–12 minutes or until golden brown.

Remove from oven. Reduce heat to 350°F.

For the Filling: In a large mixing bowl, beat eggs until foamy. Stir in melted butter, sugars and flour; mix well. Add milk, vanilla and pecans. Pour into the baked pie shell.

Bake for 30–40 minutes, or until the center is set.

If desired, serve with vanilla ice cream or whipped cream. Store at room temperature.

NUTRITION PER SERVING: 365 CALORIES; 22.5 FAT, 3.5 G PROTEIN, 37 G CARBS; 2.5 G DIETARY FIBER

Pumpkin Pie

PREP TIME: 20 minutes   COOK TIME: 50 minutes   SERVINGS: 8   INGREDIENTS: 10

If you want to keep it simple but classy, this pumpkin pie will meet all your expectations. It's easy to make, has a firm buttery crust and pleases the palate with a smooth and creamy texture.

INGREDIENTS

Pastry for Single-Crust Pie:

1½ cups all-purpose gluten-free flour blend

¼ teaspoon salt (omit if using salted butter)

½ cup butter (1 stick), cold

4–5 tablespoons of cold milk

For the Filling:

1 (16 oz.) can pumpkin purée (not pie filling)

⅔ cup granulated sugar

1½ teaspoons ground cinnamon

½ teaspoon ground nutmeg

3 eggs

½ cup milk

⅔ cup evaporated milk

OPTIONAL INGREDIENTS

vanilla ice cream, whipped cream

METHOD

Preheat oven to 375°F (190°C). Position the oven rack in center of oven.

For the Crust: In a medium mixing bowl, combine flour and salt. With a pastry knife, cut butter into flour. Add milk and combine. Add additional milk if needed. Dough should be moist and easy to roll.

Roll dough out on a gluten-free floured surface with a rolling pin until approximately 10″ in diameter.

Place dough into 9″ pie pan and trim edges if necessary. Bake for 10–12 minutes or until golden brown. Remove from oven; set aside. Reduce heat to 350°F (180°C).

For the Filling: In a large mixing bowl, combine pumpkin, sugar, cinnamon and nutmeg. Add eggs and beat until combine. Gradually stir in milk and evaporated milk. Mix well. Pour filling into pie shell. Cover the edges of the pie shell with foil to keep from overcooking.

Bake for 25 minutes, remove foil from edges and bake for additional 25 minutes or until center is firm. Cool on a wire rack.

If desired, serve with vanilla ice cream or whipped cream. Store at room temperature or in the refrigerator.

> **BAKER'S NOTE:**
> Handle the pie crust dough as little as possible to prevent a tough crust.

Strawberry Cream Cheese Pie

PREP TIME: 30 minutes   COOK TIME: 12 minutes   SERVINGS: 12   INGREDIENTS: 10

I brought this pie to work one day and set it out on the counter around 7:00 a.m. I passed by about 20 minutes later and a group of people were polishing it off. I heard one of them say "I think it's home-made—yum!" This pie is just the right amount of sweet and can be enjoyed any time of the day.

INGREDIENTS

Pastry for Single-Crust Pie:

1½ cups all-purpose gluten-free flour blend

¼ teaspoon salt (omit if using salted butter)

½ cup butter (1 stick), cold

4–5 tablespoons of cold milk

For the Filling:

3 pints of fresh strawberries

1 cup granulated sugar

3 tablespoons gluten-free corn starch

½ cup water

8 oz. cream cheese

OPTIONAL INGREDIENTS

vanilla ice cream, whipped cream

METHOD

Preheat oven to 375°F (190°C). Position the oven rack in center of oven.

For the Crust: In a medium mixing bowl, combine flour and salt. With a pastry knife, cut butter into flour. Add milk and combine. Add additional milk if needed. Dough should be moist and easy to roll. Roll dough out on a gluten-free floured surface with a rolling pin until approximately 10'' in diameter.

Place dough into 9'' pie pan and trim edges if necessary. Bake for 10–12 minutes or until golden brown. Remove from oven; set aside.

For the Filling: Remove stems from strawberries and cut into pieces into a small bowl, then mash the strawberries. In a medium saucepan, combine sugar and cornstarch. Stir in water and mashed strawberries. Cook over medium heat, stirring constantly until the mixture begins to boil. Boil for one minute, and then remove from heat. Let it cool for 10–15 minutes.

With an electric mixer, beat cream cheese until smooth. Spread cream cheese into bottom of cooked pastry shell. Pour the strawberry mixture over the top. Refrigerate for 2–3 hours. Serve cold. If desired, serve with vanilla ice cream or whipped cream.

> **BAKER'S NOTE:**
> I recommend using fresh strawberries for this recipe. If you use frozen strawberries, make sure they are completely defrosted before you add them to the mixing bowl.

Chocolate Pie Crust

PREP TIME: 10 minutes   COOK TIME: 10 minutes   SERVINGS: 12   INGREDIENTS: 4

Sweet, but not too sweet, this chocolate crust works well for many types of pies and tarts. You can use a recipe from this book or create your own masterpiece with this crust as the foundation.

INGREDIENTS

1 cup all-purpose gluten-free flour blend

¼ cup granulated sugar

¼ cup unsweetened cocoa powder

½ cup butter (1 stick), softened

> SUBSTITUTION SOLUTIONS:
> Substitute the butter with a dairy-free butter to make this pie crust dairy-free!

METHOD

Preheat oven to 325°F (165°C). Position the oven rack in center of oven.

In a medium mixing bowl, combine flour, sugar and cocoa powder. Using a pastry blender, cut in the butter until the mixture resembles fin crumbs.

Form mixture into one big ball.

Knead until smooth.

Press dough evenly into the bottom and up the sides of an 8" or 9" glass pie pan.

Bake for 12–15 minutes, or until firm in the center.

Remove from the oven and cool on a wire rack.

> BAKER'S NOTE:
> To keep the kitchen a little cleaner, I like to roll the pie crust between two pieces of wax paper. When you have it rolled out to approximately 10 inches, you can trim the edges if desired and peel it off right into the pie plate.

NUTRITION PER SERVING: 130 CALORIES; 8 FAT, 1.8 G PROTEIN, 13.8 G CARBS; 1 G DIETARY FIBER

Classic Pie Crust

PREP TIME: 10 minutes   COOK TIME: 10 minutes   SERVINGS: 12   INGREDIENTS: 4

This is your basic, classic, butter, flaky pie crust. My mother-in-law was enjoying a pot pie I made with this crust, and said it was "the best crust" she'd ever had. I smiled as I told her it was gluten-free. The family now uses this gluten-free pie crust recipe in all their gluten-free baking.

INGREDIENTS

1½ cups all-purpose gluten-free flour blend

¼ teaspoon salt (omit if using salted butter)

½ cup butter (1 stick), cold

4–5 tablespoons of cold milk

SUBSTITUTION SOLUTIONS:
Substitute the milk with almond or rice milk and the butter with a dairy-free butter to make this pie crust dairy-free!

METHOD

Preheat oven to 350°F (180°C). Position the oven rack in center of oven.

In a medium mixing bowl, combine flour and salt. With a pastry knife, cut butter into flour. Add milk and combine. Add additional milk if needed. Dough should be moist and easy to roll.

Roll dough out on a gluten-free floured surface with a rolling pin until approximately 10″ in diameter.

Place dough into pie pan and trim edges if necessary.

Bake for 10–12 minutes or until golden brown.

Remove from oven.

BAKER'S NOTE:
To keep the kitchen a little cleaner, I like to roll the pie crust between two pieces of wax paper. When you have it rolled out to approximately 10 inches, you can trim the edges if desired and peel it off right into the pie plate.

NUTRITION PER SERVING: 130 CALORIES; 8 FAT, 1.5 G PROTEIN, 13.5 G CARBS; 1 G DIETARY FIBER

Mock Graham Pie Crust

PREP TIME: 10 minutes   COOK TIME: 10 minutes   SERVINGS: 12   INGREDIENTS: 6

If I had to pick one recipe I created or re-created, this is my number-one favorite. This mock graham cracker crust is simply amazing! It is so easy to make and a perfect substitute for any recipe that calls for a graham cracker crust.

INGREDIENTS

½ cup all-purpose gluten-free flour blend

½ cup gluten-free quick cooking oats

⅓ cup brown sugar, packed

¼ teaspoon cinnamon

¼ teaspoon baking soda

¼ cup butter (½ stick), cold, cut into 1-inch cubes

> SUBSTITUTION SOLUTIONS:
> Substitute the butter with a dairy-free butter to make this pie crust dairy-free!

METHOD

Preheat oven to 350°F (180°C). Position the oven rack in center of oven.

In a food processor, combine flour, quick oats, brown sugar, cinnamon, baking soda and butter and process until finely chopped (Approximately 30 seconds).

Press pie crust mixture into the bottom of an 8″ glass pie pan. Bake for 10–12 minutes or until it starts to brown.

Remove from the oven. Crust will appear raised. It should flatten on its own. If it doesn't, press the crust with a spoon until it is even and flat.

> BAKER'S NOTE:
> If you don't have a food processor, mix the dry crust ingredients in a bowl and cut butter in until it's fine and resembles coarse crumbs.

NUTRITION PER SERVING: 154 CALORIES; 8 FAT, 1.5 G PROTEIN, 19 G CARBS; 1 G DIETARY FIBER

Cookies

Butterscotch Tassies

Chewy Chocolate Chip Cookies

Chocolate Drop Cookies

Chocolate Pressed Butter Cookies

Chocolate Filled Macadamia Cookies

Chocolate Mint Cookies

Cinnamon Almond Crescent Cookies

Coconut Macaroons

Colossal Cookies

Cranberry Scones

Cream Cheese Cookies

English Tea Cakes

Flourless Peanut Butter Cookies

Gingersnaps

Lemon Cookies

Nutmeg Cookies

Oatmeal Butterscotch Chews

Pumpkin Pecan Tassies

Russian Tea Cakes

Shortbread Cookies

Sugar Cookies

Snickerdoodles

Spritz Cookies

White Chocolate Chip Macadamia Cookies

Butterscotch Tassies

PREP TIME: 15 minutes   COOK TIME: 25 minutes   SERVINGS: 24   INGREDIENTS: 8

These buttery rich pastries complement any cup of coffee or tea. Having a dinner party soon? Lay out a batch of these tasty treats on your favorite platter and you have yourself a winning centerpiece!

INGREDIENTS

For the Pastry:

½ cup butter (1 stick), softened

3 oz. cream cheese, room temperature

1 cup all-purpose gluten-free flour blend

For the Filling:

½ cup gluten-free butterscotch chips

¼ cup gluten-free chocolate chips

2 tablespoons butter

1 tablespoon granulated sugar

1 egg

METHOD

Preheat oven to 325°F (165°C). Position the oven rack in center of oven.

For the Pastry: In a medium mixing bowl, combine butter and cream cheese. Beat until smooth and creamy. Add flour; beat on low speed until combined. Shape dough into 24 balls. Press each ball evenly and up the sides of 24 ungreased mini muffin cups; set aside.

For the Filling: In small saucepan, combine butterscotch chips, chocolate chips and butter. Heat and stir over low heat until melted. Remove from heat. Whisk in sugar and egg.

Spoon the chocolate butterscotch mixture evenly into the pastry shells, filling ⅔ of the way full.

Bake for 22–25 minutes or until the pastry is golden brown and the filling is puffed.

Remove the pan from the oven and let the tassies cool in the pan on a wire rack. Once cooled, carefully remove the tassies from the pan.

Place cookies between sheets of wax paper in an airtight container.

Store at room temperature.

NUTRITION PER SERVING: 233 CALORIES; 16 G FAT, 3 G PROTEIN, 19 G CARBS; 1 G DIETARY FIBER

Chewy Chocolate Chip Cookies

PREP TIME: 10 minutes   COOK TIME: 12 minutes   SERVINGS: 24   INGREDIENTS: 9

It took years to find the right combination of ingredients to make the chewy and moist chocolate chip cookie that my family loves. These soft, flexible and scrumptious cookies are a true classic.

INGREDIENTS

2½ cups all-purpose gluten-free flour blend

1 teaspoon baking soda

1 teaspoon xanthan gum or psyllium husk powder

1 cup of salted butter (2 sticks), melted

¼ cup granulated sugar

1¼ cups brown sugar, packed

2 eggs

1 teaspoon gluten-free vanilla extract

1½ cups gluten-free chocolate chips

METHOD

Preheat oven to 375°F (190°C). Position the oven rack in center of oven. Line two cookie sheets with parchment paper; set aside.

In a medium mixing bowl, combine flour, baking soda and xanthan gum; set aside.

In a separate large mixing bowl, mix melted butter, sugars, eggs and vanilla until combined. Continue to mix on medium for 1 minute. Gradually beat in flour mixture. Stir in chocolate chips.

Chill the dough in the refrigerator for one hour or until firm.

Shape dough into 2-oz. balls (rounded tablespoons) and drop onto the parchment-lined cookie sheet, 6 cookies per sheet.

Bake for 10–12 minutes, rotating the pans halfway through for even baking, until the cookies are light brown and slightly firm to the touch.

Remove from the oven and let cool on the cookie sheet for 2–3 minutes. Finish cooling on a wire rack. Store cookies in an airtight container.

> BAKER'S NOTE:
> If the cookie dough is not refrigerated, the butter will not set up and the cookies will flatten when baked. If you refrigerate the dough too long, the cookies will not spread when baked. If you find that the cookie dough has been refrigerated too long, leave the bowl out on the counter for a while until the dough softens.

NUTRITION PER SERVING: 253 CALORIES; 12 G FAT, 2.5 G PROTEIN, 33 G CARBS; 1 G DIETARY FIBER

Chocolate Drop Cookies

PREP TIME: 20 minutes   COOK TIME: 12 minutes   SERVINGS: 24   INGREDIENTS: 9

These soft, cake-like cookies are rich in flavor and don't fall short on texture. You can easily double this recipe for parties or visitors.

INGREDIENTS

¼ cup salted butter (½ stick), softened

½ cup granulated sugar

1 egg

1½ teaspoons gluten-free vanilla extract

3 oz. unsweetened chocolate or gluten-free semi-sweet chocolate chips, melted

½ cup all-purpose gluten-free flour blend

¼ teaspoon gluten-free baking powder

½ teaspoon xanthan gum or psyllium husk powder

1 cup chopped walnuts or pecans

SUBSTITUTION SOLUTIONS:

Substitute the butter with dairy-free butter and the chocolate chips with gluten-free, dairy-free chocolate chips to make these cookies dairy-free!

METHOD

Preheat oven to 350°F (180°C). Position the oven rack in center of oven. Line a cookie sheet with parchment paper; set aside.

In a large mixing bowl, cream the butter and sugar.

Beat in egg and vanilla. Stir in melted chocolate. In a separate medium mixing bowl, combine flour, baking powder and xanthan gum.

Gradually add flour mixture to wet mixture. Stir in nuts. Drop by rounded teaspoonfuls two inches apart onto cookie sheets.

Bake for 8–10 minutes or until the edges are firm. Remove cookies from the oven and let cool on the pan.

Once completely cooled, remove from the pan. Store in an airtight container.

Chocolate Pressed Butter Cookies

PREP TIME: 20 minutes   COOK TIME: 14 minutes   SERVINGS: 24   INGREDIENTS: 6

These cookies are great for holidays. You can dress them up with your favorite frosting, add some color with sprinkles, or serve them plain with a glass of milk. The decorating options outweigh the time it takes to make these wonderful little cookies.

INGREDIENTS

½ cup butter (1 stick), softened

¼ cup granulated sugar

½ teaspoon gluten-free vanilla extract

1¼ cups all-purpose gluten-free flour blend

½ teaspoon xanthan gum or psyllium husk powder

9 oz. gluten-free chocolate chips

SUBSTITUTION SOLUTIONS:
Substitute the butter with dairy-free butter and the chocolate chips with gluten-free, dairy-free chocolate chips to make these cookies dairy-free!

METHOD

Preheat oven to 350°F (180°C). Position the oven rack in center of oven. Line a cookie sheet with parchment paper; set aside.

In a large mixing bowl, cream the butter, sugar and vanilla. In a separate small mixing bowl, combine the flour and xanthan gum. Gradually add flour mixture to the wet mixture. Continue to mix until combined. Shape dough into 24 1-inch balls.

Place dough balls one inch apart onto an ungreased cookie sheet. Using the end of a wooden spoon handle, make a wide indentation in the center of each ball; fill the center of each indentation with 5 chocolate chips.

Bake for 12–14 minutes or until light brown. Let cool for 5 minutes. Finish cooling on wire rack. Store cookies in an air-tight container.

NUTRITION PER SERVING: 119 CALORIES; 7 G FAT, 1 G PROTEIN, 13 G CARBS; .5 G DIETARY FIBER

Chocolate-Filled Macadamia Cookies

PREP TIME: 20 minutes   COOK TIME: 14 minutes   SERVINGS: 24   INGREDIENTS: 7

My mother used to make these cookies for the holidays when I was young. We looked forward to biting into them to find a surprise of chocolate in the middle. It's almost like having two treats in one—yum!

INGREDIENTS

½ cup butter (1 stick), softened

¼ cup powdered sugar, plus extra for coating cookies

½ teaspoon gluten-free vanilla extract

½ teaspoon xanthan gum or psyllium husk powder

1¼ cups all-purpose gluten-free flour blend

4 oz. macadamia nuts, coarsely chopped

6 oz. gluten-free chocolate chips

SUBSTITUTION SOLUTIONS:

Substitute the butter with dairy-free butter and the chocolate chips with gluten-free, dairy-free chocolate chips to make these cookies dairy-free!

METHOD

Preheat oven to 350°F (180°C). Position the oven rack in center of oven.

In a medium mixing bowl, cream butter, sugar and vanilla. In a separate small mixing bowl, combine the xanthan gum and flour. Gradually add flour mixture to the wet mixture. Continue to mix until combined. Stir in macadamia nuts; set aside.

Shape teaspoonfuls of dough around 3–4 chocolate chips. They should be in the center and be completely covered. Place the round cookie balls two inches apart onto a cookie sheet.

Bake for 12–14 minutes or until lightly browned. Let cool for 10 minutes. Roll in powdered sugar until evenly coated.

Let sit for another 5 minutes and roll in powdered sugar once more. Finish cooling on wire rack.

Store cookies in an airtight container.

Chocolate Mint Cookies

PREP TIME: 20 minutes   COOK TIME: 10 minutes   SERVINGS: 36   INGREDIENTS: 10

Whomever discovered the combination of chocolate and mint was a genius. Maybe chocolate and mint should be in its own judging category at the county fair? These cookies melt in your mouth and satisfy your sweet tooth.

INGREDIENTS

½ cup salted butter (1 stick)

3 oz. unsweetened chocolate or gluten-free semi-sweet chocolate chips

½ cup granulated sugar

½ cup brown sugar, packed

1 egg

¼ cup buttermilk

1 teaspoon peppermint extract

1¾ cups all-purpose gluten-free flour blend

½ teaspoon gluten-free baking powder

¼ teaspoon baking soda

> **SUBSTITUTION SOLUTIONS:**
> Substitute the butter with dairy-free butter, substitute the chocolate chips with gluten-free, dairy-free chocolate chips and the buttermilk with ½ cup rice or soy milk and 2 teaspoons of vinegar (let sit until thickened) to make these cookies dairy-free!

METHOD

Preheat oven to 350°F (180°C). Position the oven rack in center of oven. Line a cookie sheet with parchment paper; set aside.

On the stove in a small saucepan, or in the microwave in a small bowl, melt butter and chocolate together.

In a large mixing bowl, beat sugars, egg, buttermilk and peppermint extract. Add in melted chocolate mixture and beat until smooth.

In a separate medium mixing bowl, combine flour, baking powder and baking soda. Gradually add to wet mixture. Place dough in the refrigerator for 20–25 minutes until the dough starts to firm.

Drop by tablespoonfuls, three inches apart, onto cookie sheet. Bake for 8–10 minutes or until edges are firm. Let cool for 10 minutes before removing from the cookie sheet. Finish cooling on wire rack.

Cookies will be fragile until completely cooled.

Store in an airtight container.

Cinnamon Almond Crescent Cookies

PREP TIME: 20 minutes   COOK TIME: 12 minutes   SERVINGS: 36   INGREDIENTS: 7

You know when you put cinnamon and almonds together you get an award-winning combination that will sure to be a favorite with the family. These buttery, spicy cookies are great at picnics, parties or by the fireplace. What I am saying is you can pretty much eat them anytime and be happy.

INGREDIENTS

1 cup butter (2 sticks), softened

⅓ cup granulated sugar, plus ¼ cup sugar for dipping cookies

½ teaspoon gluten-free vanilla extract

2½ cups all-purpose gluten-free flour blend

1 teaspoon xanthan gum or psyllium husk powder

½ cup almond meal

½ teaspoon cinnamon for dipping cookies

> **SUBSTITUTION SOLUTIONS:**
> Substitute the butter with dairy-free butter to make these cookies dairy-free!

METHOD

Preheat oven to 350°F (180°C). Position the oven rack in center of oven. Line a cookie sheet with parchment paper; set aside.

In a large mixing bowl, cream butter, ⅓ cup sugar and vanilla.

In a separate small mixing bowl, combine flour, xanthan gum and almond meal. Gradually add flour mixture to wet mixture, mixing until combined.

Roll dough into 36–42 1-inch balls. Shape dough balls into crescents.

Place 12 crescents two inches apart onto the cookie sheet. Bake for 10–12 minutes or until set, not brown. Let cool for 10 minutes on cookies sheet. Cookies will be fragile until completely cooled.

For Sugar Topping: In a small mixing bowl, combine ¼ cup of sugar and the cinnamon. Roll warm crescents in cinnamon sugar. Place on wire racks until cool. Store in an airtight container.

NUTRITION PER SERVING: 94 CALORIES; 6 G FAT, 1 G PROTEIN, 9.5 G CARBS; .5 G DIETARY FIBER

Coconut Macaroons

PREP TIME: 20 minutes   COOK TIME: 20 minutes   SERVINGS: 24   INGREDIENTS: 7

You really have to like coconut to understand just how wonderful these cookies are. These thick, dense, chewy cookies—dipped in chocolate—will rival most candy bars. I recommend enjoying them in moderation.

INGREDIENTS

2½ cups packaged flaked coconut (about 7 oz.)

⅔ cup granulated sugar

⅓ cup all-purpose gluten-free flour blend

¼ teaspoon salt

3 egg whites, slightly beaten

½ teaspoon almond extract (you can use vanilla extract)

¼ cup gluten-free chocolate chips

> **SUBSTITUTION SOLUTIONS:**
> Substitute gluten-free chocolate chips with gluten-free, dairy-free chocolate chips to make these cookies dairy-free!

METHOD

Preheat oven to 325°F (165°C). Position the oven rack in center of oven. Line a cookie sheet with parchment paper; set aside.

In a medium mixing bowl, combine coconut, sugar, flour and salt. Stir in egg whites and almond extract.

Drop coconut cookie dough by the tablespoon, two inches apart, onto the cookie sheet. Bake for 18–20 minutes or until the edges are golden brown.

Remove from the oven and let cool on the cookie sheet for 2–3 minutes. Carefully remove the cookies from the cookie sheet and finish cooling on a wire rack. Save your parchment-covered cookie sheet.

Over low heat on the stove, or in the microwave 30 seconds at a time, slowly melt chocolate chips. Dip the bottoms of the cooled cookies in the chocolate, letting excess drip off.

Place the cookies back on the parchment paper cookie sheet, chocolate side up, until cooled completely. If desired, drizzle melted chocolate on the tops. Let cool completely, then store cookies in an airtight container.

> **BAKER'S NOTE:**
> The faster you use your eggs, the less time any potential bacteria will have to multiply. When properly handled, you can refrigerate egg yolks in a sealed container for 2 to 4 days. Yolks don't usually freeze well. Save the egg yolks from this recipe for a later date and you can use them to make key lime pie!

Colossal Cookies

PREP TIME: 20 minutes   COOK TIME: 10 minutes   SERVINGS: 30   INGREDIENTS: 9

There are so many recipes out there for monster cookies and colossal cookies. I am pretty picky with the combination of texture and flavors. These will give you just a little bit of a crunch and a little bit of chew. You can easily play with the cooking time to achieve your favorite texture.

INGREDIENTS

¼ cup butter (½ stick), softened

¾ cup granulated sugar

¾ cup brown sugar, packed

2 eggs

½ teaspoon vanilla extract

1 cup chunky peanut butter

1¼ teaspoons baking soda

3 cups gluten-free rolled oats

1 cup gluten-free chocolate chips

SUBSTITUTION SOLUTIONS:
Substitute the butter with dairy-free butter and the chocolate chips with gluten-free, dairy-free chocolate chips to make these cookies dairy-free!

METHOD

Preheat oven to 350°F (180°C). Position the oven rack in center of oven. Line a cookie sheet with parchment paper; set aside.

In a large mixing bowl, cream butter, sugars, eggs and vanilla. Add peanut butter and baking soda; beat well. Stir in oats and chocolate chips.

Drop by ¼ cup, two to three inches apart, onto cookie sheet. Flatten to approximately 2½ inches in diameter.

Bake for 10–12 minutes until light brown and slightly firm to the touch. Remove from the oven and let cool on the cookie sheet for 3–5 minutes. Finish cooling on a wire rack. Store in an airtight container.

Cranberry Scones

Scones! Who doesn't love a scone? Scones are the love child of a cookie and a cake. Maybe that's why they are sometimes referred to as a tea cake. Either way, just about any scone is welcome on my plate.

INGREDIENTS

1¾ cups all-purpose gluten-free flour blend

3 tablespoons granulated sugar

2½ teaspoons gluten-free baking powder

1 teaspoon xanthan gum or psyllium husk powder

⅓ cup butter, cold

1 egg

¾ cup milk, plus 2 tablespoons for the top

½ cup dried cranberries

2 tablespoons granulated sugar

OPTIONAL INGREDIENTS

lemon curd, butter

METHOD

Preheat oven to 400°F (200°C). Position the oven rack in center of oven. Line a cookie sheet with parchment paper; set aside.

In a large mixing bowl, combine flour, sugar, baking powder and xanthan gum. With a pastry knife, cut in the butter until it resembles crumbs. Add egg and ¾ cup milk and combine.

On a gluten-free floured surface, knead cranberries into the dough. Separate the dough into 8 individual scones. Round and shape dough into circles approximately 1 inch thick and place on cookie sheet. Brush the top of each scone with milk and sprinkle with sugar.

Bake for 15–18 minutes or until light brown and the center is firm to touch. Remove from the oven and cool on a wire rack. If desired, serve with lemon curd or butter. Store in an airtight container.

> **BAKER'S NOTE:**
> Want to change these up a little? Add 1 teaspoon of cinnamon to your flour mixture and substitute raisins for the dried cranberries!

Cream Cheese Cookies

PREP TIME: 20 minutes   COOK TIME: 14 minutes   SERVINGS: 24   INGREDIENTS: 9

Cream cheese provides cookies and cakes with an extra rich cheese-like flavor. These cookies are moist, rich and delicate, but packed with flavor and satisfaction.

INGREDIENTS

½ cup shortening

4 oz. cream cheese, room temperature

½ cup granulated sugar

1 teaspoon salt

1 egg yolk

1 teaspoon gluten-free vanilla extract

1 cup all-purpose gluten-free flour blend

1 teaspoon xanthan gum or psyllium husk powder

24 candied cherries or candied pineapple pieces

METHOD

Preheat oven to 350°F (180°C). Position the rack in center of oven. Line a cookie sheet with parchment paper; set aside.

In a medium mixing bowl, cream shortening, cream cheese, sugar and salt. Add in egg yolk and vanilla. Mix until combined.

In a separate small mixing bowl, combine flour and xanthan gum. Gradually add the flour mixture to the wet mixture until combined.

Drop by rounded teaspoonfuls, two inches apart, onto the cookie sheet. Top each with a piece of candied cherry or pineapple.

Bake for 12–14 minutes, or until light brown and slightly firm to the touch.

Remove from the oven and let cool on the cookie sheet for 1–2 minutes. Finish cooling on a wire rack. Store cookies in an airtight container.

English Tea Cakes

PREP TIME: 20 minutes   COOK TIME: 14 minutes   SERVINGS: 36   INGREDIENTS: 6

Okay, hands down, these are my absolute favorite cookies. There was no way I was going to leave these out! These cookies are so rich and buttery, I have to limit myself to two or I go into a butter coma.

INGREDIENTS

1 cup butter (2 sticks), softened

½ cup granulated sugar

1 teaspoon gluten-free vanilla extract

2 cups all-purpose gluten-free flour blend

2 teaspoons xanthan gum or psyllium husk powder

36 pecans, toasted

> **SUBSTITUTION SOLUTIONS:**
> Substitute the butter with dairy-free butter to make these cookies dairy-free!

METHOD

Preheat oven to 350°F (180°C). Position the oven rack in center of oven. Grease a 36 mini-muffin cup pan and set aside.

In a large mixing bowl, cream butter, sugar and vanilla until smooth. In a separate medium mixing bowl, combine flour and xanthan gum. Gradually add flour mixture to wet mixture, continue to mix until well combined.

Drop by tablespoonfuls into the mini muffin cups; flatten slightly. Press a pecan into the center of each cup.

Bake for 12–14 minutes until edges are light brown and center is set. Cool completely in the pan. Carefully twist the cookies as you remove them from the pan. Store in an airtight container.

Flourless Peanut Butter Cookies

PREP TIME: 10 minutes   COOK TIME: 10 minutes   SERVINGS: 24   INGREDIENTS: 4

This recipe is an oldie but a goodie. I, of course, didn't dream up this recipe, but I wanted to include it because so many people who are gluten-free don't realize these are made with ingredients that are naturally gluten-free and are inexpensive to make.

INGREDIENTS

1 cup peanut butter

1 cup granulated sugar

1 egg, lightly beaten

1 teaspoon gluten-free vanilla extract

METHOD

Preheat oven to 325°F (165°C). Position the oven rack in center of oven. Line a cookie sheet with parchment paper; set aside.

In a medium bowl, mix the peanut butter, sugar, egg and vanilla until well combined. Spoon 1 tablespoon of mixture about two inches apart onto the cookie sheet. Flatten the mounds with a fork, making a crosshatch pattern on the cookies.

Bake for 8–10 minutes or until the edges are golden brown. Remove from the oven and let the cookies cool on the pan for 3–5 minutes. Transfer to a wire cooling rack until completely cool.

Gingersnaps

You could easily enjoy these spicy, cruncy and delicious cookies with a cup of your favorite hot beverage and be content. Double the recipe and save some cookies for your pumpkin cheese-cake crust? Just thinking ahead.

INGREDIENTS

¾ cup shortening

1 cup granulated sugar

1 egg

¼ cup molasses

2 cups all-purpose gluten-free flour blend

2 teaspoons baking soda

1½ teaspoons ground ginger

1 teaspoon ground cinnamon

½ teaspoon salt

granulated sugar for rolling cookies

METHOD

Preheat oven to 350°F (180°C). Position the oven rack in center of oven. Line a cookie sheet with parchment paper; set aside.

In a large mixing bowl, cream shortening, sugar, egg and molasses.

In a separate medium mixing bowl, combine flour, baking soda, ginger, cinnamon and salt. Gradually add flour mixture to the wet mixture until combined.

Roll the dough into teaspoon-size balls. Dip one side of the dough balls into sugar and place sugar side up onto the cookie sheet two inches apart.

Bake for 12–15 minutes or until lightly brown and starting to crack. Carefully transfer cookies to a wire rack and cool. Store in an airtight container.

Lemon Cookies

PREP TIME: 10 minutes   COOK TIME: 12 minutes   SERVINGS: 36   INGREDIENTS: 10

Have you heard of the phrase, "easy, peasy, lemon squeezey?" That pretty much sums up these cookies. They are easy to make. They please just about anyone with taste buds. And you literally use a lemon.

INGREDIENTS

2 teaspoons lemon juice

⅓ cup milk

½ cup butter (1 stick)

¾ cup granulated sugar

1 egg

1 teaspoon finely shredded lemon peel

1¾ cup all-purpose gluten-free flour blend

1 teaspoon gluten-free baking powder

¼ teaspoon baking soda

1 teaspoon xanthan gum or psyllium husk powder

SUBSTITUTION SOLUTIONS:
Substitute the butter with dairy-free butter and the milk with rice, soy or almond milk to make these cookies dairy-free!

METHOD

Preheat oven to 350°F (180°C). Position the oven rack in center of oven. Line two cookie sheets with parchment paper; set aside.

In a small mixing bowl or cup, stir two teaspoons lemon juice into the milk and set aside for five minutes.

In a medium mixing bowl, beat butter, sugar, egg, lemon peel and lemon milk mixture.

In a separate medium mixing bowl, combine flour, baking powder, baking soda and xanthan gum.

Add the flour mixture to the wet mixture and beat until combined.

Drop by rounded teaspoons two inches apart onto an ungreased cookie sheet. Bake for 10–12 minutes or until the edges are light brown. Transfer cookies to a wire rack and cool.

If desired, frost each cookie with powdered sugar icing (page 161). Store in an airtight container.

Nutmeg Cookies

PREP TIME: 10 minutes   COOK TIME: 10 minutes   SERVINGS: 60   INGREDIENTS: 10

Nutmeg is a very strong spice—I always tell my fellow bakers to use it with caution. This recipe provides just enough nutmeg to trick your taste buds into thinking they're eating a donut-flavored cookie. Who doesn't like donuts or cookies? Win!

INGREDIENTS

1 cup butter (two sticks), softened

¾ cup granulated sugar

½ cup powdered sugar

1 egg

1 teaspoon gluten-free vanilla extract

2½ cups all-purpose gluten-free flour blend

1 teaspoon xanthan gum or psyllium husk powder

½ teaspoon baking soda

½ teaspoon cream of tartar

1 teaspoon ground nutmeg

SUBSTITUTION SOLUTIONS:
Substitute the butter with dairy-free butter to make these cookies dairy-free!

METHOD

Preheat oven to 350°F (176°C). Position the oven rack in center of oven. Line two cookie sheets with parchment paper; set aside.

In a medium mixing bowl, cream butter, sugars, egg and vanilla. Beat until combined.

In a separate medium mixing bowl combine flour, xanthan gum, baking soda, cream of tartar and nutmeg. Add the flour mixture to wet mixture and mix until well combined. Refrigerate for one hour.

Shape dough into 60 1-inch balls. Place 12 balls onto the cookie sheet 2 inches apart. Flatten with a glass dipped in sugar.

Bake for 10–12 minutes or until the edges are light brown. Transfer cookies to a wire rack and cool. Store in an airtight container.

Oatmeal Butterscotch Chews

PREP TIME: 20 minutes   COOK TIME: 9 minutes   SERVINGS: 48   INGREDIENTS: 10

Yes, this recipe is for oatmeal butterscotch chews. I know you're still in shock because you're salivating and your stomach just gurgled. They are a true match. Move forward with caution.

INGREDIENTS

1¼ cups all-purpose gluten-free flour blend

1 teaspoon baking soda

½ teaspoon ground cinnamon

1 cup of butter (2 sticks), softened

¾ cup granulated sugar

¾ cup brown sugar, packed

2 eggs

1 teaspoon gluten-free vanilla extract

3 cups gluten-free rolled oats

1½ cups gluten-free butterscotch chips

METHOD

Preheat oven to 375°F (190°C). Position the oven rack in center of oven. Line two cookie sheets with parchment paper; set aside.

In a medium mixing bowl, combine flour, baking soda and cinnamon; set aside.

In a separate medium bowl, beat butter, sugars, eggs and vanilla. Gradually beat in flour mixture. Stir in oats and butterscotch chips.

Drop by rounded tablespoons onto cookie sheets. Bake for 8–10 minutes until the edges appear brown and the center starts to firm.

Remove from the oven and let cool on the cookie sheet for 3–5 minutes. Slide the parchment paper onto a wire rack. Finish cooling on a wire rack. Store in an airtight container.

NUTRITION PER SERVING: 136 CALORIES; 6 G FAT, 2 G PROTEIN, 17.5 G CARBS; 1 G DIETARY FIBER

Pumpkin Pecan Tassies

PREP TIME: 30 minutes   COOK TIME: 40 minutes   SERVINGS: 24   INGREDIENTS: 10

These little mini pie–like cookies are fabulous. They have just a hint of pumpkin, a tad bit of spice and a smidgen of crunch. I could eat these by the handful—hence, I only make them when company is over.

INGREDIENTS

For the Pastry:

½ cup butter, softened

3 oz. cream cheese, softened

1 cup all-purpose gluten-free flour blend

For the Filling:

½ cup, plus ¼ cup packed brown sugar

¼ cup pumpkin purée (not pie filling)

2 tablespoons butter, softened and divided

1 egg yolk

1 teaspoon gluten-free vanilla extract

⅛ teaspoon ground cinnamon

⅛ teaspoon ground nutmeg

½ cup chopped pecans

> **BAKER'S NOTE:**
> If you don't have a mini-muffin pan, you can use a regular 12-serving muffin pan. Shape the dough into 12 balls and press evenly and up the sides of each muffin cup.

METHOD

Preheat oven to 325°F (135°C). Position the oven rack in center of oven.

For the Pastry: In a medium mixing bowl, beat butter and cream cheese until smooth and creamy. Add flour; beat on low speed until combined.

Shape dough into 24 1-inch balls. Press each ball evenly and up the sides of mini-muffin cup pan. Bake for 8–10 minutes or until edges are light brown. If you don't have a mini-muffin pan, see the baker's note below.

For the Filling: In a medium mixing bowl, combine ½ cup brown sugar, pumpkin, 1 tablespoon butter, egg yolk, vanilla, cinnamon and nutmeg. Spoon the filling evenly into the warm cups.

In a small mixing bowl, combine remaining ¼ cup of brown sugar, 1 tablespoon butter and chopped pecans, sprinkle over the filling in each cup.

Bake for an additional 23–25 minutes or until set and the pastry is golden brown.

Remove from the oven and let cool in the pan on a wire rack for 10 minutes. Carefully remove the tassies from the pan and finish cooling on a wire rack. Store in an airtight container.

NUTRITION PER SERVING: 138 CALORIES; 9.5 G FAT, 1.5 G PROTEIN, 12 G CARBS; 1 G DIETARY FIBER

Russian Tea Cakes

PREP TIME: 30 minutes   COOK TIME: 20 minutes   SERVINGS: 36   INGREDIENTS: 7

You know those little ball-shaped cookies dipped in powdered sugar that have been super popular at holiday gatherings the past 40 years? Yes, this recipe produces those little mouthwatering, palate-satisfying cookies, and they're gluten-free!

INGREDIENTS

1 cup butter (2 sticks), softened

1 teaspoon gluten-free vanilla extract

½ cup powdered sugar

2¼ cups all-purpose gluten-free flour blend

1 teaspoon xanthan gum or psyllium husk powder

1 cup chopped walnuts or pecans

½ cup powdered sugar for decoration

> **SUBSTITUTION SOLUTIONS:**
> Substitute the butter with dairy-free butter to make these cookies dairy-free!

METHOD

Preheat oven to 400°F (200°C). Position the oven rack in center of oven.

In a medium mixing bowl, cream butter and vanilla until smooth.

In a separate medium mixing bowl, combine the ½ cup powdered sugar, flour and xanthan gum. Gradually stir flour mixture into the butter mixture until just blended. Stir in the chopped nuts.

Roll dough into 1-inch balls, and place them two inches apart on an ungreased cookie sheet.

Bake for 18–20 minutes until set but not brown. Immediately remove from the cookie sheet to a wire rack. Cool cookies for 5 minutes, then roll in powdered sugar.

After 5 minutes, roll the cookies in powdered sugar a second time. Cool completely.

Store in an airtight container.

Shortbread Cookies

PREP TIME: 20 minutes   COOK TIME: 20 minutes   SERVINGS: 24   INGREDIENTS: 4

Shortbread cookies are traditionally a Christmas cookie that blends butter, sugar and flour to make a rich yet delicate cookie. I like to serve them all year long with coffee, tea or lemonade. They are easy to make and versatile.

INGREDIENTS

¾ cup butter (1 stick, plus ½ stick), softened

¼ cup granulated sugar

2 cups all-purpose gluten-free flour blend

1 teaspoon xanthan gum or psyllium husk powder

METHOD

Preheat oven to 350°F (180°C). Position the oven rack in center of oven. Line two cookie sheets with parchment paper; set aside.

In a medium mixing bowl, cream the butter and sugar. In a separate medium mixing bowl, combine flour and xanthan gum.

Stir flour mixture into the butter mixture until just combined. If dough is crumbly, mix in an additional 1–2 table-spoons of softened butter.

Knead dough four to five times and roll into one big ball.

On a lightly gluten-free floured surface, roll dough out until ½ inch thick. Cut into small shapes by hand using cookie cutters or a glass.

Place cookies one inch apart on cookie sheet. Bake for 12–14 minutes or until light brown around the edges. Let the cookies cool for 5 minutes on the pan, then remove the parchment paper to a wire rack. Once cool, store in an airtight container.

Snickerdoodles

What do you get when you combine the flavors of butter, sugar and cinnamon? A snickerdoodle! Just saying the word "snickerdoodle" is fun. These chewy and crunchy cookies are big, flat, round and marvelously flavored.

INGREDIENTS

½ cup butter (1 stick)

1 cup granulated sugar, plus 2 tablespoons sugar for rolling cookies

1 egg

½ teaspoon gluten-free vanilla extract

1½ cups all-purpose gluten-free flour blend

1 teaspoon xanthan gum or psyllium husk powder

¼ teaspoon baking soda

¼ teaspoon cream of tartar

1 teaspoon of ground cinnamon for rolling cookies

> **SUBSTITUTION SOLUTIONS:**
> Substitute the butter with dairy-free butter to make these cookies dairy-free!

METHOD

Preheat oven to 350°F (180°C). Position the oven rack in center of oven. Line two cookie sheets with parchment paper; set aside.

In a medium mixing bowl, beat butter, 1 cup sugar, egg and vanilla until combined.

In a separate medium mixing bowl, combine flour, xanthan gum, baking soda and cream of tartar and mix until combined. Add the flour mixture to the wet mixture and beat until combined. Cover and chill for 1 hour.

Once dough is chilled and firm, shape dough into 1-inch balls.

Combine the remaining two tablespoons of sugar and cinnamon. Roll balls in sugar and cinnamon mixture. Place two inches apart onto the cookie sheet. Using the bottom of a glass, gently flatten each cookie to about ½ inch thick.

Bake for 10–12 minutes or until the edges are light brown. Transfer cookies to a wire rack and cool. Store in an airtight container.

Spritz Cookies

PREP TIME: 20 minutes   COOK TIME: 9 minutes   SERVINGS: 48   INGREDIENTS: 7

Super simple, buttery and delicate, these cookies are a true classic. They are easy to make, fun to press and a big hit with kids.

INGREDIENTS

½ cup butter (1 stick), softened

4 oz. cream cheese, room temperature

½ cup brown sugar, packed

½ teaspoon gluten-free vanilla extract

¼ teaspoon salt (omit if using salted butter)

1½ cups all-purpose gluten-free flour blend

½ teaspoon xanthan gum or psyllium husk powder

OPTIONAL INGREDIENTS

colored sugar or sprinkles

METHOD

Preheat oven to 375°F (190°C). Position the oven rack in center of oven. Line two cookie sheets with parchment paper; set aside.

In a medium mixing bowl, cream butter, cream cheese, brown sugar, vanilla and salt.

In a separate medium mixing bowl, combine flour and xanthan gum. Add flour mixture to wet mixture. Stir until combined.

Using a cookie press, press 12 cookies one inch apart onto cookie sheet. If desired, sprinkle with colored sugar.

Bake for 7–9 minutes until light brown. Remove from the oven and let cool on the cookie sheet for 2 minutes. Finish cooling on a wire rack. Store cookies in an airtight container.

Sugar Cookies

PREP TIME: 10 minutes   COOK TIME: 8 minutes   SERVINGS: 24   INGREDIENTS: 9

These sugar cookies are fluffy, moist and can be described as a vanilla cupcake in the shape of a cookie. I like to frost mine and leave them overnight before diving into them. I make them at least once a month and color the frosting to match the month or holiday in which they are being enjoyed.

INGREDIENTS

⅔ cup shortening

¾ cup granulated sugar

1 teaspoon gluten-free vanilla extract

1 egg

4 teaspoons of milk

2 cups all-purpose gluten-free flour blend

1½ teaspoons gluten-free baking powder

¼ teaspoon salt

1 teaspoon of xanthan gum or psyllium husk powder

SUBSTITUTION SOLUTIONS:
Substitute the butter with dairy-free butter to make these cookies dairy-free!

METHOD

Preheat oven to 375°F (190°C). Position the oven rack in center of oven. Line two cookie sheets with parchment paper; set aside.

In a medium mixing bowl, cream shortening, sugar, vanilla and egg. Stir in the milk.

In a separate bowl, mix the flour, baking powder, salt and xanthan gum. Make sure to mix well to evenly distribute the ingredients.

Gradually add the dry ingredients to the wet ingredients until combined.

Roll dough into 1½-inch balls, or use a rounded tablespoon. Place the dough balls onto the cookie sheet two inches apart. Press each one down with the bottom of a cup until the cookie is round and approximately ½ inch thick.

Bake for 8–10 minutes until light brown. Remove from the oven and let cool on the cookie sheet for 5 minutes. Using a spatula, carefully remove the cookies from the cookie sheet to a cooling rack.

Finish cooling on a wire rack. Once completely cool, frost with butter cream or cream cheese frosting. Store cookies in an airtight container.

BAKER'S NOTE:
If your dough seems too dry, try leaving out ¼ cup of the dry mixture or adding a couple extra teaspoons of milk.

White Chocolate Macadamia Nut Cookies

PREP TIME: 15 minutes	COOK TIME: 12 minutes	SERVINGS: 36	INGREDIENTS: 10

If the name doesn't say it all, I don't know what else will convince you to make these wonderful cookies. I like to leave mine a little undercooked for a gooey delicious treat.

INGREDIENTS

1¼ cups whole macadamia nuts, toasted

½ butter (1 stick), softened

½ cup granulated sugar

½ cup brown sugar, packed

1 egg

1 teaspoon gluten-free vanilla extract

1½ cups all-purpose gluten-free flour blend

½ teaspoon baking soda

½ teaspoon salt (omit if using salted butter)

1 cup gluten-free vanilla chips

METHOD

Preheat oven to 350°F (180°C). Position the oven rack in center of oven. Line two cookie sheets with parchment paper; set aside.

Chop ½ cup of macadamia nuts and set aside. Melt 2 tablespoons of the butter. In a food processor, combine melted butter and remaining macadamia nuts. Process until the mixture forms a lumpy paste. Set aside.

In a medium bowl, cream the remaining six tablespoons of butter. Beat in sugars, egg and vanilla. Continue to beat until light and fluffy. Beat in the macadamia nut paste.

In a separate medium mixing bowl, combine the chopped macadamia nuts, flour, baking soda and salt. Add flour mixture to wet mixture and mix until combined. Stir in vanilla chips.

Drop by rounded tablespoonfuls, two inches apart, onto the cookie sheet.

Bake for 10–12 minutes, rotating the pans halfway through for even baking, until the cookies are light brown and slightly firm to the touch. Remove from the oven and let cool on the cookie sheet for 2–3 minutes.

Finish cooling on a wire rack. Store cookies in an airtight container.

Brownies and Bars

Brownies

Butterscotch Bars

Cheesecake Bars

Chocolate Chip Granola Bars

Fruit-Filled Oatmeal Squares

Fudge Brownies

Lemon Bars

Mocha Fudge Brownies

Orange Brownies

Turtle Bars

Brownies

PREP TIME: 10 minutes   COOK TIME: 30 minutes   SERVINGS: 24   INGREDIENTS: 9

These rich, moist and chewy brownies are easy to make and quick to bake. After one brownie you'll leave the kitchen wondering if you should have doubled the batch.

INGREDIENTS

1¼ cups granulated sugar

¾ cup butter (1½ sticks)

½ cup unsweetened cocoa

2 eggs

1 cup milk

1 teaspoon gluten-free vanilla extract

1½ cups all-purpose gluten-free flour blend

1 teaspoon gluten-free baking powder

¼ teaspoon baking soda

OPTIONAL INGREDIENTS

1 cup chopped nuts

1 cup chocolate chips

> ### SUBSTITUTION SOLUTIONS:
> Substitute the butter with dairy-free butter, the milk with coconut milk or almond milk to make these brownies dairy-free!

METHOD

Preheat oven to 350°F (180°C). Position the oven rack in center of oven. Grease a 15x10x2" pan; set aside.

In a large saucepan over low heat, melt the sugar, butter and cocoa. Once melted, remove from the heat. Stir in eggs, milk and vanilla until combined.

In a separate medium mixing bowl, combine flour, baking powder and baking soda. Add flour mixture to the sauce pan. Beat until combined. *Optional: Stir in nuts or chocolate chips if desired.*

Spread batter into the pan and bake for 25–28 minutes or until center is set and a toothpick inserted near the center comes out clean. Cool in pan on a wire rack. Frost if desired.

Cut into bars and store in an airtight container.

Butterscotch Bars

PREP TIME: 15 minutes   COOK TIME: 25 minutes   SERVINGS: 16   INGREDIENTS: 8

These butterscotch bars are a great compromise when you can't decide if you want a cookie or a brownie! Try using grated orange zest in the place of the vanilla for a citrus twist.

INGREDIENTS

¼ cup butter, melted

½ cup brown sugar, packed

½ cup granulated sugar

1 teaspoon gluten-free vanilla extract

1 egg

1 cups all-purpose gluten-free flour blend

1 teaspoon gluten-free baking powder

½ teaspoon salt (omit if using salted butter)

OPTIONAL INGREDIENTS

1 cup chopped nuts

1 cup gluten-free butterscotch chips

SUBSTITUTION SOLUTIONS:
Substitute the butter with dairy-free butter to make these bars dairy-free!

METHOD

Preheat oven to 350°F (180°C). Position the oven rack in center of oven. Grease an 8x8x2" pan; set aside.

In a medium mixing bowl, mix melted butter, brown sugar, sugar, vanilla and egg.

In a separate medium mixing bowl, combine flour, baking powder and salt. Add flour mixture to wet mixture. Stir until combined. Dough will be thick. *Optional: Stir in nuts and/or butterscotch chips if desired.*

Spread dough into the pan and bake for 28–32 minutes or until brown and the center is set. Cool in the pan on a wire rack.

Once completely cool, cut into bars and store in an airtight container at room temperature.

Cheesecake Bars

PREP TIME: 10 minutes   COOK TIME: 40 minutes   SERVINGS: 24   INGREDIENTS: 10

Cheesecake bars are sometimes superior to a traditional cheesecake, because they make portion control so much easier to manage. With a nutty and buttery crust, topped with a smooth and creamy cheesecake filling, these bars are hard to resist.

INGREDIENTS

For the Crust:

2 cups all-purpose gluten-free flour blend

⅔ cup brown sugar, packed

⅔ cup butter, cold

1 cup chopped walnuts or pecans

For the Filling:

16 oz. cream cheese, room temperature

½ cup granulated sugar

2 eggs

¼ cup milk

2 tablespoons lemon juice

1 teaspoon gluten-free vanilla extract

METHOD

Preheat oven to 350°F (180°C). Position the oven rack in center of oven. Grease a 13x9x2" pan; set aside.

For the Crust: In a medium mixing bowl, combine flour and brown sugar. With a pastry cutter, cut in butter until mixture resembles coarse crumbs. Stir in chopped walnuts or pecans. Reserve 1 cup of crumb mixture.

Press remaining crumb mixture into the bottom of the 13x9x2" pan. Bake for 10–12 minutes. Remove from the oven.

For the Filling: In a separate medium mixing bowl, beat cream cheese and sugar until smooth and creamy. Add eggs, one at a time, beating after each addition. Beat in milk, lemon juice and vanilla until well combined. Pour cream cheese mixture over the crust. Sprinkle reserved crumbs evenly over the cream cheese mixture in pan.

Bake for additional 25–30 minutes or until the edges are light brown and filling is set. Cool in pan on a wire rack.

Cut into 24 bars and store in an airtight container in the refrigerator.

> **BAKER'S NOTE:**
> Avoid over-beating the batter. Over-beating incorporates additional air and tends to cause cracking on the surface.

NUTRITION PER SERVING: 230 CALORIES; 15 G FAT, 3.5 G PROTEIN, 20 G CARBS; 1.5 G DIETARY FIBER

Chocolate Chip Granola Bars

PREP TIME: 15 minutes   COOK TIME: 5 minutes   SERVINGS: 16   INGREDIENTS: 6

These granola bars are easy to make and you don't have to turn on your oven. You can pack them for lunch or a snack, or enjoy them after dinner to tame that subtle sweet tooth.

INGREDIENTS

¼ cup butter (½ stick)

¼ cup honey

⅓ cup brown sugar, packed

2 cups gluten-free quick-cooking oats

1 cup gluten-free rice crisp cereal

¼ cup gluten-free chocolate chips

> **SUBSTITUTION SOLUTIONS:**
> Substitute the butter with dairy-free butter and the chocolate chips with gluten-free, dairy-free chocolate chips to make these dairy-free!

METHOD

Grease a 9x13" pan; set aside.

In a small saucepan, over medium heat, melt butter, honey and brown sugar until it comes to a boil. Reduce the heat to low and simmer for two minutes, stirring frequently. Remove from heat.

In a medium mixing bowl, combine oats and rice crispy cereal. Pour wet ingredients over dry ingredients and mix well to moisten all ingredients. Pour mixture into the pan and press down until it is one inch in thickness. Continue to press mixture down so that it is very compressed. Sprinkle with chocolate chips and press down lightly.

Cool in the pan on a wire rack until the chocolate chips are set. Cut into bars. Store at room temperature.

Fruit-Filled Oatmeal Squares

PREP TIME: 15 minutes   COOK TIME: 30 minutes   SERVINGS: 24   INGREDIENTS: 6

This kid-friendly, fruit-filled bar is inexpensive to make and only has six ingredients! The combination of the flavors from the oats and brown sugar leaves the palate with a nutty aftertaste. You can use any flavor of fruit jam or multiple flavors to mix it up.

INGREDIENTS

1 cup all-purpose gluten-free flour blend

1 cup gluten-free quick-cooking oats

⅔ cup brown sugar, packed

¼ teaspoon baking soda

½ cup butter (1 stick), cold

10-oz. jar of your favorite fruit jam (I like to use strawberry, raspberry or plum.)

> SUBSTITUTION SOLUTIONS:
> Substitute the butter with dairy-free butter to make these dairy-free!

METHOD

Preheat oven to 350°F (180°C). Position the oven rack in center of oven. Grease 9x9x2" pan; set aside.

In a medium mixing bowl combine flour, oats, brown sugar and baking soda. Cut in butter until the flour mixture looks crumbly. Reserve half of the crumbly flour mixture for the topping.

Press the remaining flour mixture into the bottom of the pan. Spread fruit jam on top. Sprinkle with remaining flour mixture.

Bake for 30–35 minutes or until the top is golden brown. Remove the pan from the oven and cool on a wire rack. Cut into 24 bars. Store in an airtight container at room temperature.

Fudge Brownies

PREP TIME: 10 minutes   COOK TIME: 30 minutes   SERVINGS: 16   INGREDIENTS: 6

Rich, fudgy, smooth and creamy are only a few of the adjectives you can use to describe these delicious brownies. Like most brownies, you can add your favorite optional ingredients to this recipe to yield monster results.

INGREDIENTS

½ cup butter (1 stick)

2 oz. unsweetened chocolate

1 cup granulated sugar

2 eggs

1 teaspoon gluten-free vanilla extract

¾ cup all-purpose gluten-free flour blend

OPTIONAL INGREDIENTS

½ cup chopped nuts

> SUBSTITUTION SOLUTIONS:
> Substitute the butter with dairy-free butter to make these brownies dairy-free!

METHOD

Preheat oven to 350°F (180°C). Position the oven rack in center of oven. Grease an 8x8x2" square pan; set aside.

Stirring frequently, melt the butter and chocolate in a medium saucepan over low heat. Remove from the heat. Stir in sugar, eggs and vanilla until combined. Stir in the flour. *Optional: Stir in the chopped nuts if desired.*

Spread batter into the pan and bake for 30 minutes or until center is set.

Cool on a wire rack. Frost if desired. Cut into bars. Store in an airtight container at room temperature.

Lemon Bars

PREP TIME: 15 minutes   COOK TIME: 40 minutes   SERVINGS: 16   INGREDIENTS: 7

I love lemon bars. They are refreshing, tart and inviting. I have served them at summer picnics and at holiday parties. With only seven ingredients, you have a delightful bar with a crumbly shortbread-like crust and tangy lemon filling.

INGREDIENTS

For the Crust:

⅓ cup butter

¼ cup granulated sugar

1 cup all-purpose gluten-free flour blend

For the Lemon Layer:

2 eggs

¾ cup granulated sugar

2 tablespoons all-purpose gluten-free flour blend

2 teaspoons shredded lemon zest

3 tablespoons lemon juice

¼ teaspoon gluten-free baking powder

OPTIONAL INGREDIENTS

powdered sugar

METHOD

Preheat oven to 350°F (180°C). Position the oven rack in center of oven. Grease an 8x8x2" pan; set aside.

For the Crust: In a medium mixing bowl, beat the butter with an electric mixer for 30 seconds. Add ¼ cup of the sugar and beat until combined. Add 1 cup of flour and beat until crumbly. Press the flour mixture into the bottom of the pan. Bake in the oven for 18–20 minutes or just until golden brown.

For the Lemon Layer: In a medium mixing bowl, combine eggs, the remaining ¾ cup sugar, 2 tablespoons flour, lemon zest, lemon juice and baking powder. Beat for one minute on high. Pour over hot baked crust.

Bake an additional 20 minutes, until light brown and the center is set. Cool on a wire rack. *Optional: When cool, if desired, sift powdered sugar over the top.* Store in an airtight container in the refrigerator.

Mocha Fudge Brownies

PREP TIME: 10 minutes   COOK TIME: 40 minutes   SERVINGS: 24   INGREDIENTS: 9

Just reading the ingredients for this recipe makes me salivate. You have seen me use the words creamy, fudge-like and rich. Add mocha somewhere in the middle and you have yourself a brownie masterpiece.

INGREDIENTS

For the Crust:

⅓ cup butter

¼ cup granulated sugar

1 cup all-purpose gluten-free flour blend

For the Filling:

1 14-oz. can sweetened condensed milk

½ cup unsweetened cocoa powder

1 egg

¼ cup all-purpose gluten-free flour blend

1 teaspoon gluten-free vanilla extract

2 tablespoons of coffee or coffee flavoring

½ teaspoon gluten-free baking powder

OPTIONAL INGREDIENTS

½ cup chopped nuts (pecans or walnuts work best)

METHOD

Preheat oven to 350°F (180°C). Position the oven rack in center of oven. Grease an 8x8x2" pan; set aside.

For the Crust: In a medium mixing bowl, beat the butter with an electric mixer for 30 seconds. Add ¼ cup of the sugar and beat until combined. Add 1 cup of flour and beat until crumbly. Press the flour mixture into the bottom of the pan. Bake in the oven for 18–20 minutes or just until golden brown.

For the Filling: In a large mixing bowl, combine sweetened condensed milk, cocoa, egg, ¼ cup of flour, vanilla extract, coffee and baking powder, mix well. *Optional: Stir in nuts if desired.*

Spread mocha mixture on prepared crust and bake for 20 minutes or until the center is set. Cool pan on a wire rack. Frost if desired. Cut into bars and store at room temperature.

Orange Brownies

PREP TIME: 20 minutes   COOK TIME: 32 minutes   SERVINGS: 16   INGREDIENTS: 10

Have you seen the picture for these orange brownies yet? Warning, the picture is known to increase saliva flow and oven temperatures. This moist, cake-like brownie is full of the delicious natural flavors of orange and cocoa. Convinced yet?

INGREDIENTS

For the Brownies:

½ cup butter (1 stick)

½ cup unsweetened cocoa

2 eggs

1 cup granulated sugar

¾ cup all-purpose gluten-free flour blend

½ cup chopped pecans

From 1 large orange: 2 tablespoons orange juice, 1 tablespoon grated orange peel

⅛ teaspoon salt

For the Frosting:

2 cups powdered sugar

3 tablespoons butter

2 tablespoons orange juice

1 tablespoon grated orange peel

> **SUBSTITUTION SOLUTIONS:**
> Substitute the butter with dairy-free butter to make these brownies dairy-free!

METHOD

Preheat oven to 350°F (180°C). Position the oven rack in center of oven. Grease an 8x8x2" pan; set aside.

In a small sauce pan melt butter and cocoa until smooth. Remove from the heat.

In a medium mixing bowl, beat eggs until frothy. Add sugar, flour, pecans, orange juice, peel and salt. Beat until combined. Add cocoa mixture and mix well.

Pour batter into the pan. Bake for 28–32 minutes or until edges begin to pull away from the sides of the pan. Remove from the oven and cool on a wire rack.

For the Frosting: In a medium mixing bowl, beat the powdered sugar, butter, orange juice and peel. Beat until smooth and creamy. Spread evenly over the cooled brownies.

Cut into bars. Store in an airtight container at room temperature.

Turtle Bars

These three-layer gluten-free buttery treats, partnered with your favorite glass of milk, will make the ending to any day memorable. The moment the buttery crumbly crust topped with caramel and chocolate enters your watering mouth, your palate is sure to send relay messages back to your brain that ultimate satisfaction has been achieved.

INGREDIENTS

For the Crust:

½ cup butter (1 stick)

2 cups all-purpose gluten-free flour blend

1 cup brown sugar, packed

1 cup pecan pieces

For the Caramel Layer:

⅔ cup butter

½ cup brown sugar, packed

For the Topping:

1 cup gluten-free chocolate chips

METHOD

Preheat oven to 350°F (180°C). Position the oven rack in center of oven.

For the Crust: Using a pastry blender or fork, in a medium mixing bowl combine ½ cup butter, flour and 1 cup brown sugar until the mixture forms fine crumbs. Press the mixture into an ungreased 9x13x2" pan. Sprinkle the crust with the pecan pieces; set aside.

For the Caramel Layer: Combine ⅔ cup butter and ½ brown sugar in a medium saucepan and bring to a boil over medium heat, stirring constantly. Continue to boil for 1 minute.

Drizzle the caramel mixture evenly over the crust. Bake for 20 minutes. Remove from the oven.

For the Topping: Immediately after removing the crust from the oven, sprinkle it with chocolate chips. Allow the chocolate chips to stand for 5–10 minutes so that they will melt. Using the back of a spoon spread the chocolate evenly over the surface of the bars. Let the bars cool completely before cutting. Store in an airtight container at room temperature.

Frostings

Chocolate Butter Cream Frosting

Chocolate Sour Cream Frosting

Cream Cheese Frosting

Powdered Sugar Icing

Vanilla Butter Cream Frosting

Whipped Cream Cheese Frosting

Chocolate Butter Cream Frosting

PREP TIME : 10 minutes   SERVINGS: Enough to frost 24 cupcakes   INGREDIENTS: 5

Delicious on most cakes, sugar cookies and brownies. You can make this frosting dairy-free by using alternative milks such as almond milk or rice milk and using butter substitutes.

INGREDIENTS

½ cup butter (1 stick), room temperature

½ cup unsweetened cocoa powder

1½ teaspoons gluten-free vanilla extract

4½ cups powdered sugar

¼ cup milk

SUBSTITUTION SOLUTIONS:

Substitute the milk for almond, rice, or coconut milk and the butter for dairy-free butter to make this frosting dairy-free!

METHOD

In a medium mixing bowl, beat butter and vanilla until smooth and creamy. Add cocoa powder and beat until combined. Gradually add powdered sugar, one cup at a time. Slowly beat in the milk. Beat in additional milk if needed, to obtain desired consistency.

You can store frosting in the refrigerator in a sealed container for up to a week.

NUTRITION PER SERVING: 131 CALORIES; 4 G FAT, .5 G PROTEIN, 24 G CARBS; 0 G DIETARY FIBER

Chocolate Sour Cream Frosting

PREP TIME : 15 minutes   SERVINGS: Enough to frost 24 cupcakes   INGREDIENTS: 4

Full of flavor and stacking up to its reputation, this rich and creamy fudge-like frosting is a favorite on brownies, cookies and cakes.

INGREDIENTS

1 cup gluten-free chocolate chips

¼ cup butter, room temperature

½ cup sour cream

2½ cups powdered sugar

METHOD

In a saucepan, melt chocolate and butter over low heat, stirring frequently until completely melted. Remove from the stovetop right away and cool for 5 minutes. Stir in the sour cream. Gradually add powdered sugar, beating until smooth. Serve right away.

You can store frosting in the refrigerator in a sealed container for up to a week.

NUTRITION PER SERVING: 129 CALORIES; 5.5 G FAT, 1 G PROTEIN, 19 G CARBS; 1 G DIETARY FIBER

Cream Cheese Frosting

PREP TIME : 10 minutes   SERVINGS: Enough to frost 24 cupcakes   INGREDIENTS: 4

I grew up spreading cream cheese frosting on sugar cookies. Some of my favorite combinations with cream cheese frosting include chocolate cake, carrot cake and red velvet cake.

INGREDIENTS

8 oz. cream cheese, room temperature

½ cup butter (1 stick), room temperature

2 teaspoons gluten-free vanilla extract

4½ cups powdered sugar

METHOD

In a medium mixing bowl, beat together cream cheese, butter and vanilla until light and fluffy. Gradually add powdered sugar, one cup at a time, beating well.

You can store frosting in the refrigerator in a sealed container for up to a week.

NUTRITION PER SERVING: 154 CALORIES; 7 G FAT, 1 G PROTEIN, 23 G CARBS; 0 G DIETARY FIBER

Powdered Sugar Icing

PREP TIME : 5 minutes   SERVINGS: 1 cup of icing   INGREDIENTS: 3

Do you need a quick and easy icing for your donuts, bundt cakes or cookies? With only three ingredients, this recipe is an old classic but a sure winner. You can add additional character to the icing with juice lemon, orange juice, or by switching up the flavored extract.

INGREDIENTS

2 cups powdered sugar

½ teaspoon gluten-free vanilla extract
(or your favorite extract)

¼ cup milk

METHOD

In a medium mixing bowl, beat together butter and vanilla until smooth and creamy. Gradually add powdered sugar, one cup at a time, beating well. Alternate one cup of powdered sugar and 1 tablespoon of milk until all ingredients are blended. Beat in additional milk if needed to obtain desired constancy.

You can store icing in the refrigerator in a sealed container for up to a week.

NUTRITION PER SERVING: 986 CALORIES; .5 G FAT, 2 G PROTEIN, 243 G CARBS; 0 G DIETARY FIBER

Vanilla Butter Cream Frosting

PREP TIME : 10 minutes   SERVINGS: Enough to frost 24 cupcakes   INGREDIENTS: 4

Vanilla butter cream frosting is one of the most versatile frostings and it is so easy to make. You can leave it thick for easy decorating by adding less milk, or add additional milk for a rich and buttery icing.

INGREDIENTS

½ cup butter (1 stick), room temperature

1½ teaspoons gluten-free vanilla extract

4½ cups powdered sugar

¼ cup milk

> **SUBSTITUTION SOLUTIONS:**
> Substitute the milk for almond, soy, rice, or coconut milk and the butter for dairy-free butter to make this frosting dairy-free!

METHOD

In a medium mixing bowl, beat together butter and vanilla until smooth and creamy. Gradually add powdered sugar, one cup at a time, beating well. Alternate one cup of powdered sugar and 1 tablespoon of milk until all ingredients are blended. Beat in additional milk if needed to obtain desired constancy.

   You can store frosting in the refrigerator in a sealed container for up to a week.

NUTRITION PER SERVING: 124 CALORIES; 3.5 G FAT, 0 G PROTEIN, 22.5 G CARBS; 0 G DIETARY FIBER

Whipped Cream Cheese Frosting

PREP TIME : 10 minutes   SERVINGS: Enough to frost 24 cupcakes   INGREDIENTS: 4

This delightful cream cheese frosting is just sweet enough to complement any cupcake or cake. Adding heavy cream provides extra structure, body and flavor. You get the best of both worlds with the sweetness from the cream cheese and lightness of whipped cream.

INGREDIENTS

1 cup heavy whipping cream

1 8-oz. package cream cheese

1½ cups powdered sugar

1 teaspoon gluten-free vanilla extract

METHOD

In a small mixing bowl, beat whipping cream until stiff peaks form; set aside.

   In a large bowl combine cream cheese, sugar and vanilla. Beat until smooth; fold in whipped cream.

   You can store frosting in the refrigerator in a sealed container for up to a week.

NUTRITION PER SERVING: 87 CALORIES; 5.5 G FAT, 1 G PROTEIN, 8.5 G CARBS; 0 G DIETARY FIBER

RESOURCES

Arrowhead Mills
www.arrowheadmills.com
(800) 434-4246

Bob's Red Mill Natural Foods
Gluten-free flours and xanthan gum
www.bobsredmill.com
(800) 349-2173

Carnation
Gluten-free sweetened condensed milk and evaporated milk
www.verybestbaking.com/Carnation.aspx
(800) 854-8935

Enjoy Life
Chocolate Chips
www.enjoylifefoods.com

Hain Pure Foods
Gluten-free baking powder
www.hainpurefoods.com
(866) 595-8917

Hershey
Gluten-free baking chips (check out their gluten-free list)
www.thehersheycompany.com
(800) 437-7439